Education for Equality

EDUCATION
FOR
EQUALITY

WOMEN'S RIGHTS PERIODICALS
AND
WOMEN'S HIGHER EDUCATION
1849-1920

Patricia Smith Butcher

LIBRARY

CONTRIBUTIONS IN WOMEN'S STUDIES, NUMBER 111

Greenwood Press
NEW YORK · WESTPORT, CONNECTICUT · LONDON

Library of Congress Cataloging-in-Publication Data

Butcher, Patricia Smith.
    Education for equality : women's rights periodicals and women's
higher education, 1849–1920 / Patricia Smith Butcher.
       p. cm.—(Contributions in women's studies, ISSN 0147–104X ;
no. 111)
    Bibliography: p.
    Includes index.
    ISBN 0–313–25940–2 (lib. bdg. : alk. paper)
    1. Women—Education (Higher)—United States—History. 2. Women's
rights—United States—History. 3. Feminist literature. 4. Women's
periodicals, American. I. Title. II. Series.
LC1756.B92   1989
376'.65'09034—dc20   89-11874

British Library Cataloguing in Publication Data is available.

Library of Congress Catalog Card Number: 89–11874
ISBN: 0–313–25940–2
ISSN: 0147–104X

First published in 1989

Greenwood Press, Inc.
88 Post Road West, Westport, Connecticut   06881

Printed in the United States of America

∞

The paper used in this book complies with the
Permanent Paper Standard issued by the National
Information Standards Organization (Z39.48–1984).

10 9 8 7 6 5 4 3 2 1

CONTENTS

ACKNOWLEDGMENTS

Researching and writing a book are arduous tasks, but the assistance of many kind and generous individuals eased the process considerably. I was aided by Joan Burstyn, an outstanding adviser, a true teacher, and the consummate role model for all women in academia.

In the classes of David Carr, James Giarelli, and William L. O'Neill, I honed the idea for the project. They encouraged my early efforts and were generous scholars who offered constructive criticism.

Librarians and staff of the Roscoe L. West Library at Trenton State College are frequently commended for their strong service orientation and willingness to assist researchers. During my time "on the other side of the reference desk," I have been the grateful recipient of their skills, speed, and friendly words of encouragement. From personal experience I know why librarians appear in so many book acknowledgments. Their assistance and research talents can never be praised enough.

This study owes much to the support of the Trenton State College Faculty and Institutional Research and Sabbatical Leave Committee. Their awards of financial assistance and release time over the past six years were well-used and deeply appreciated.

I dedicate this book to my husband, John. With love and gratitude, I thank him for his endless support, patience, and good humor through these long years of writing.

INTRODUCTION

A painter once exhibited to a lion, a splendid picture in which
Hercules was represented conquering the Nemean lion, who lay
prostrate and bleeding at his feet. After examining it steadfastly
for some time, the king of the beasts exclaimed haughtily—"This
is all very well, but if lions were painters, we should see the other
side of the picture."

Aesop's Fables

Women's rights papers assumed the role to which Aesop's lion
aspired. By chronicling women's efforts to attain equality, the
papers portrayed "the other side of the picture" to receptive
supporters as well as to those who found the presentation
disruptive and distressing. Relentless catalysts, women's rights
papers assisted in the evolution, dramatization, and celebration
of new roles for women.

Amid the torrent of issues addressed by the papers, women's
right to higher education was especially prominent. Contending
that females had an inalienable right to self-development, wom-
en's rights activists proclaimed that dissident message through
their press. For seventy years, women's rights papers recounted

the entwined histories of women's education and women's struggle for equal rights.

To many, the women's rights movement and the passage of the Nineteenth Amendment, which granted women suffrage, are synonymous. Although winning women's right to vote was a momentous accomplishment, the women's rights movement embraced a far richer spectrum of goals. Many of them, such as women's right to higher education, have remained unexamined and, consequently, unknown.

The intense struggle for higher education by a small number of middle-class American women from 1849 to 1920 merits analysis. This book links two little-known aspects of the women's rights movement, its press and its aspirations for women's higher education. By exploring the theme of women's higher education as it appeared in eleven women's rights papers, one gains insights into the collective mind of the women's rights movement, which labored to shape a new version of womanhood between 1849 and 1920. The papers conceived, articulated, dramatized, and celebrated the vision of educated women who would enjoy a life of equality and dignity.

Women's rights activists proclaimed their right to higher education in the 1848 Declaration of Sentiments. With the sentence: "He has denied her the faculties for obtaining a through education, all colleges being closed against her," the plucky group of reformers challenged prevailing social norms and irrevocably linked education to women's equality.

Increasingly fearful that educated women would forsake their traditional domestic duties and encroach upon the male sphere, the popular press of the nineteenth and early twentieth centuries publicized the notion that women's unique mental and physiological traits rendered them incapable of education and destined them solely for the world confined by parlor, nursery, and kitchen. Opposition to women's education took many guises over the decades. The most gripping arguments were those laden with scientific findings derived from biology, physiology, medicine, and, later, eugenics.[1] All focused around three issues: women's health would suffer if they pursued intellectual endeavors; women were incapable of learning because their brains were too small; and education would deter them from marital and maternal responsibilities.

Headlines such as "The Intellectual Inferiority of Women," "Death from Overstudy," "High Education Cause of Physical Decay in Women," and "College Women and Race Suicide" warned society that serious academic work would destroy female minds and bodies and would irrevocably damage the well-being of the nation. The press ridiculed women's ventures into higher education, challenged their intellectual capacities, and demeaned their ambitions to utilize their newly acquired learning.

Fortunately a more balanced, supportive, and accurate record of women's intellectual abilities and educational accomplishments exists within women's rights papers. The papers redefined women's role and forged new paths for educated women. They provided socially and geographically isolated women with information, role models, advice, and encouragement available nowhere else. Written by women, for women, the papers strove to reshape women's lives by promoting higher education.

This analysis studies a representative sample of the many women's rights papers published. The eleven titles were selected because they were among the best-known, were geographically diversified, represented the seven decades of the first women's rights movement, and because they covered the broad spectrum of women's rights rather than concentrating on the single issue of suffrage. Their reporting on women's advances in higher education raises a number of questions: What was the relationship between women's higher education and the women's rights movement? Were there differences among the papers because of variations in time and place of publication? Did the papers alter their coverage of higher educational issues between 1849 and 1920? Did philosophical differences within the women's movement influence the papers' views on how and why women should be educated? Were the papers influential?

This book adds some missing links to histories of women's higher education and the women's rights movement. A rich legacy of the women's rights movement, the papers were mirrors and molders of women's lives. As they promoted and chronicled new lifestyles and intellectual endeavors for women, they left a provocative, vivid, and highly personal view of women's higher education.

NOTE

1. For a review of arguments against educating women, see Susan Phinney Conrad, *Perish the Thought: Intellectual Women in Romantic America, 1830–1860* (New York: Oxford University Press, 1976); Barbara Welter, "Anti-Intellectualism and the American Woman: 1800–1860," *Mid-America* 48 (October 1966):258–270; Carroll Smith-Rosenberg and Charles Rosenberg, "The Female Animal: Medical and Biological Views of Woman and Her Role in Nineteenth-Century America," *Journal of American History* 60 (September 1973):332–356; Elizabeth Fee, "Nineteenth-Century Crainiology: The Study of the Female Skull," *Bulletin of the History of Medicine* 53 (Fall 1979):415–433; Joan Burstyn, *Victorian Education and the Ideal of Womanhood* (Totowa, N.J.: Barnes & Noble Books, 1980); Louise Michele Newman, ed., *Men's Ideas/Women's Realities: Popular Science, 1870–1915* (New York: Pergamon Press, 1985); and Cynthia Eagle Russett, *Sexual Science: the Victorian Construction of Womanhood* (Cambridge: Harvard University Press, 1989).

LIST OF WOMEN'S RIGHTS
PERIODICALS USED

Periodical	Place of Publication	Dates
Agitator	Chicago, Ill.	1869
Lily	Seneca Falls, N.Y. Mount Vernon, Ohio Richmond, Ind.	1849–56
New Northwest	Portland, Oreg.	1871–87
Pioneer	San Francisco, Calif.	1869–73
Queen Bee	Denver, Colo.	1882–95
Revolution	New York, N.Y.	1868–70
Una	Providence, R.I. Boston, Mass.	1853–55
Woman's Advocate	Philadelphia, Pa.	1855–56?
Woman's Chronicle	Little Rock, Ark.	1888–93

Woman's Journal	Boston, Mass.	1870–1932
Woman Citizen	New York, N.Y.	
Woman's Tribune	Beatrice, Nebr. Washington, D.C. Portland, Ore.	1883–1909

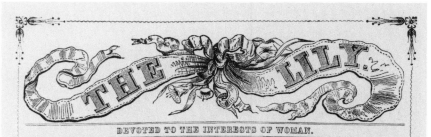

THE LILY.

DEVOTED TO THE INTERESTS OF WOMAN.

AMELIA BLOOMER,   EDITOR AND PUBLISHER.

VOL. 4.   SENECA FALLS, N. Y., AUGUST, 1852.   NO. 8.

DARE TO STAND ALONE.

BY FRANCES D. GAGE.

Be firm, be bold, be strong, be true,
  And "dare to stand alone;"
Strive for the right whate'er ye do,
  Though helpers there be none.

Nay, bend not to the swelling surge
  Of popular sneer and wrong;
'T will bear thee on to ruin's verge,
  With current wild and strong.

Stand for the Right! Humanity
  Implores with groans and tears,
Thine aid to break the festering links
  That bind her toiling years.

Stand for the Right! Though falsehood reign,
  A poisoned arrow cannot wound
A conscience pure and clear.

Stand for the Right!—and with clean hands
  Exalt the truth on high;
Thou 'lt find warm, sympathizing hearts
  Among the passers-by—

Men who have seen, and thought, and felt,
  Yet could not boldly dare
The battle's brunt, but by thy side
  Will every danger share.

Stand for the Right!—proclaim it loud—
  Thou 'l't find an answering tone
In honest hearts, and thou no more
  Be doomed to stand alone!

The following address, written by Miss Ann Preston, and designed for adoption by the Convention as an exposition of its principles and purposes, was impressively read by the author at the Woman's Rights Convention at Westchester, Pa.

ADDRESS.

The question is repeatedly asked by those who have thought but little upon the subject of woman's position in society, "What does woman want more than she possesses already? Is she not beloved, honored, guarded, cherished?—Wherein are her rights infringed, or her liberties curtailed?"

Glowing pictures have been drawn of the fitness of the present relations of society, and of the beauty of woman's dependence upon the protecting love of man; and frightful visions have been evoked of the confusion and perversion of nature which would occur if the doctrine of the equal rights of man and woman was once admitted.

The idea seems to prevail that movements for the elevation of woman arise not from the legitimate wants of society, but from the vague restlessness of unquiet spirits; not from the serene dictates of wisdom, but from the headlong impulses of fanaticism.

We came not here to argue the question of the relative strength of intellect in man and woman, for the reform which we advocate depends not upon its settlement.

We place not the interests of woman in antagonism to that of her brother, for

"The woman's cause is man's.
  They rise or sink together,
Dwarfed or God-like, bond or free."

We maintain not that woman should lose any of that refinement and delicacy of spirit which, as a celestial halo, ever encircles the pure in heart.

We contend not that she shall become noisy and dictatorial, and abjure the quiet graces of life.

We claim not that she, any more than her brother, should engage in any vocation, or appear in any situation to which her nature and abilities are not fitted.

But we ask for her, as for man, equality before the law, and freedom to exercise all her powers and faculties under the direction of her own judgment and volition.

When a woman dies leaving behind her a husband and children, no appraisers come into the desolated home to examine the effects; the father is the guardian of his offspring; the family relation is not invaded by law. But when a man dies, the case is entirely different; in the hour of the widow's desolation, strangers come into the house to take an inventory of the effects, strangers are appointed to be the guardians of her children, and she, their natural caretaker, thenceforth has no legal direction of their interests; strangers decide upon the propriety of the sale of the property—earned, perhaps, by her own and her husband's mutual efforts—and her interest in the estate is coolly designated as the "widow's incumbrance!"

In the extremity of her bereavement, there is piled upon her, not only the dread of separation from her children, but that of being sent homeless from the spot where every object has been consecrated by her tenderest affections.

Nor is the practical working of this law better than its theory; all over the country there are widows who have been made doubly desolate by its provisions—widows separated from their children, who, if they had had the disposal of their own and their husband's mutual property, might have retrieved their circumstances, and kept the household band together.

We ask for such change in public sentiment as shall procure the repeal of this oppressive law.

We ask that woman shall have free access to vocations of profit and honor, the means of earning a livelihood and independence for herself! As a general rule, profitable employments are not considered open to woman, nor are her business capabilities encouraged and developed by systematic training. Gloomy must be the feelings of the father of a family of young daughters when he is about to bid farewell to the world, if he is leaving them without the means of pecuniary support. Their brothers may go out into society and gain position and competency; but for them there is but little choice of employment, and, too often, they are left with depressed and crippled energies to pine and chafe under the bitter sense of poverty and dependence.

Their pursuits are to be determined, not by their inclination, judgment, and ability, as are those of man, but by the popular estimate of what is proper and becoming. In Turkey, public delicacy is outraged if a woman appears unveiled beyond the walls of the Harem; in America a sentiment no less arbitrary presumes to chalk out for her the precise boundaries of womanly propriety; and she who ventures to step beyond them, must do it at the peril of encountering low sneers, coarse allusions, and the withering imputation of want of feminine delicacy.

Even for the same services woman generally receives less than man. The whole tendency of our customs, habits and teaching, is to make her dependent—dependent in outward circumstances, dependent in spirit.

As a consequence of her fewer resources, marriage has been to her the great means of securing position in society. Thus it is that this relation, which should ever be a "holy sacrament"—the unbiased and generous election of the free and self-sustained being, too often is degraded into a mean acceptance of a shelter from neglect and poverty!

We ask that woman shall be trained to unfold her whole nature, to exercise all her powers and faculties.

It is said that the domestic circle is the peculiar province of woman; that "men are what mothers make them." But how can that woman who does not live for self-culture and self-development, who has herself no exalted objects in life, imbue her children with lofty aspirations, or train her sons to a free and glorious manhood?

She best can fulfill the duties of wife and mother, who is fitted for other and varied usefulness. The being who lives for one relation only, cannot possess the power and scope which are required for the highest excellence even in that one. If the whole body is left without exercise, one arm does not become strong; if the tree is stunted of its growth, one branch does not shoot into surpassing luxuriance.

That woman whose habits and mental training enable her to assist and sustain her husband in seasons of difficulty, and whose children rely on her as a wise counsellor,—commands a life-long reverence far deeper and dearer than can be secured by transient accomplishments, of the most refined and delicate imbecility.

All women are not wives and mothers, but all have spirits needing development—powers that all grow with their exercise.

Amelia Bloomer, editor of the *Lily*. By permission of the Seneca Falls Historical Society.

Paulina Wright Davis, editor of the *Una*. By permission of Ayer Company Publishers, Inc.

Elizabeth Cady Stanton, editor, and Susan B. Anthony, owner and business manager, of the *Revolution*. By permission of the National Portrait Gallery, Smithsonian Institution.

Mary Rice Livermore, editor of the *Agitator*. By permission of Ayer Company Publishers, Inc.

Abigail Scott Duniway, editor of the *New Northwest*, with the first issue of the paper in 1871. By permission of David C. Duniway.

Catherine Cunningham (center), editor of the *Woman's Chronicle* with associate editors, Mrs. William Cahoon, Jr. (left) and Mrs. Mary Burt Brooks (right). By permission of Mary Burt Brooks Nash.

Clara Bewick Colby, editor of the *Woman's Tribune*. By permission of Ayer Company Publishers, Inc.

Lucy Stone, founder of the *Woman's Journal*. By permission of Ayer Company Publishers, Inc.

1

THE WOMEN'S RIGHTS
PRESS

Reclining on a chaise lounge in her boudoir, a middle-class woman of the nineteenth century could while away countless hours leafing through publications produced specifically for her. Ladies' magazines such as the *Bower of Taste, Ladies' Mirror, Godey's Lady's Book, Ladies' Magazine, Domestic Monthly,* and *The Mothers' Magazine,* decorously but determinedly defined the narrow perimeters of woman's sphere. Doyennes of women's lives, ladies' magazines venerated women's domestic role and provided devoted readers with fashion news, advice on etiquette, child-rearing practices, and edifying poetry and fiction.

Women's rights periodicals were also produced for a female audience. However, their purpose was not to amuse but to raise social awareness. Women's rights papers were not as glossy nor as prolific as the ladies's magazines and they appealed to a limited audience of women. Defying the message of "true womanhood" promoted by ladies's magazines, women's rights magazines promoted female equality through education.

Ironically, the *Lily,* the first women's rights paper, began with little concern for women's rights or their educational advancement. The *Lily* was published in Seneca Falls, New York, on

January 1, 1849—six months after the town had been the reluctant site of the First Woman's Rights Convention. The paper originated as a temperance title produced by members of the local ladies' temperance society. However, the collective enthusiasm of the group waned while preparing the first issue. When the second issue appeared in February, Amelia Jenks Bloomer, an officer of the temperance society with some journalism experience, had assumed total responsibility for producing the monthly.

Despite the *Lily's* temperance origins, material on improving women's status quickly began to vie for space with articles decrying the use of liquor. In October 1849 Bloomer authored her first editorial promoting women's rights. Subsequently, women's equality became a standard theme.

Bloomer proudly acknowledged her paper's significance to the fledgling women's rights movement and wrote: "The *Lily* was the first paper published devoted to the interests of woman and, so far as I know, the first one owned, edited and published by a woman."[1] Bloomer's claim to primacy is most likely accurate based on information gleaned from cursory accounts of the women's rights press. Whereas women owned, edited, and published antebellum periodicals, such as the *Advocate of Moral Reform* and the *Pittsburgh Saturday Visiter*, the *Lily* was the first to devote itself to promoting women's rights.[2]

In 1854 Bloomer and her paper moved to Mt. Vernon, Ohio, where the *Lily* became a semimonthly with the impressive circulation figure of 6000 copies an issue.[3] A year later Bloomer relocated farther west to Council Bluffs, Iowa. Because the town lacked adequate printing and mailing facilities, Bloomer sold the *Lily* to Mary Birdsall of Richmond, Indiana. Birdsall maintained the paper's familiar format and continued its support of women's and temperance issues. Although Bloomer announced that she would continue as a corresponding editor, by late 1855 her name disappeared from the masthead and her columns appeared less frequently. Birdsall's failing health made it difficult for her to continue the paper, and the last issue of the *Lily* appeared in December 1856.[4]

In 1853 a second women's rights title appeared. Called the *Una*, it began publication in Providence, Rhode Island. Unlike the *Lily*, the monthly was a women's rights title from its inception. Paulina

Wright Davis, a wealthy reformer, was its editor and proprietor and published the *Una* at her own expense.[5]

Davis and her paper provided a theoretical framework for the early women's rights movement. In her inaugural editorial, Davis declared that the *Una* would "discuss the rights, sphere, duty and destiny of woman fully and fearlessly." She wanted women to think. Envisioning the *Una* as an antidote to the vapid material read by most women, Davis wrote: "Women have been too well, and too long satisfied with Ladies' Books and Ladies' Magazines and Miscellanies; it is time they should have stronger nourishment; and with a work so peculiarly their own."[6]

A lively, thought-provoking publication, *Una*'s material ranged from an assessment of the political contributions of Mary Queen of Scots to the poignant diary entries of an oppressed seamstress. Book reviews and household hints appeared next to accounts of women's rights conventions, and poems by Elizabeth Barrett Browning.

To bolster the *Una's* flagging circulation, Davis transferred publication of the paper to Boston in January 1855 and named Caroline Dall, a social reformer, as coeditor. These changes extended the paper's publication for additional months. The *Una* ceased publication in October 1855 because of financial problems and a meager subscription list. In announcing the *Una's* demise, Birdsall, the *Lily's* new editor, acerbically assessed the differences between the two papers. She commented that the *Lily* "with earnest simplicity, has dealt mainly with the practical interdicts of woman, the living active wrongs that shackle her individuality, and crush her mentality, and depress her best and her strongest being,—the *Una* has dealt more with the *principles* and policy from which grow her wrongs, and in high-toned, scholastic essays, shown the grand basis of her rights."[7]

Before it ceased publication, the *Una* announced the appearance of the *Woman's Advocate,* a Philadelphia-based women's paper edited by Anne Elizabeth McDowell.[8] Somewhat skeptically, the *Una* reported that the Philadelphia paper "claims to be an independent paper, its design not to press woman's right to 'legal suffrage' but to present her wrongs and plead for their redress."[9] Unlike the avowedly middle-class audiences of the *Lily* and the *Una*, the *Woman's Advocate* dedicated itself "to the elevation of the female industrial class." The paper was true to its intended audience: a woman was its editor, its printers and typesetters were females paid the same wages as their male counterparts, and a joint stock company of women owned the paper.

Although attentive to the interests of working women, the editor did not want her paper to be labeled a women's rights title. McDowell opposed woman suffrage, refusing to "clamor for the political rights of woman." When the *Una* demanded that the *Woman's Advocate* promote woman suffrage, McDowell responded with an editorial. Written in her usual no-nonsense tone, she informed her sister publication: "Take no position! Is it no position to demand our right to life and the means wherewith to gain an honorable subsistence? Know, transcendental sisters, we differ with you. Bless your grumbling souls, our blackened hands give us more evidence of our position that will tell on the public mind than all the windy resolutions ever passed by all the mutual admiration societies in the land."[10] Although resisting the woman suffrage issue, McDowell and her paper supported other women's concerns, most notably women's right to work, to receive job training, and to earn the same wages as male workers when performing the same job.

Published as alternatives to ladies' magazines, the three early women's rights periodicals resembled each other in neither tone nor audience. The *Lily* began as a temperance title, the *Una* aspired to elevate women's intellect, and the *Woman's Advocate* appealed to working women. With their lack of conformity and interests, these antebellum titles became models for the next generation of women's rights titles.

With the emancipation of the slaves and the Civil War, interest in women's issues and women's rights papers languished. The women's rights movement as a whole went into the "doldrums" and its press did not resurface until 1870.

Three years after the Civil War's conclusion, a new phalanx of women's rights titles began to appear. Unlike their predecessors, they originated not only in the East but in large and small towns of the Midwest, Far West, and South. More geographically diverse and prolific than their antebellum sisters, the new women's rights papers were forthright and even militant in their choice of titles. Traditional women's magazines appeared under flowery appellations such as *Rose Bud* and *Lily of the Valley* or were named *Ladies' Garland*, *Ladies' Pearl*, or *Ladies' Casket*, all suitably appropriate titles for their "true women" readers. Antebellum women's rights periodicals had followed suit, with the exception of the *Woman's Advocate* whose audience was working women. Postwar women's rights periodicals, more confident of their message, rejected the floral and genteel and selected bolder names for themselves. By their titles alone—*Revolution, Agitator, Pioneer,* and *Queen Bee*—postwar women's rights periodicals asserted their mission to expand women's sphere. Other women's rights periodicals forthrightly proclaimed themselves as publications for "women" and appeared under mastheads emblazoned with titles such as *Woman's Journal*, *Woman's Chronicle*, and *Woman's Tribune*.

The *Revolution*, the first postwar women's rights publication, appeared in New York City on January 8, 1868. A resolute name, the stirring motto "Men, their rights and nothing more; women, their rights and nothing less," and the dynamic combination of Susan B. Anthony as owner/business manager and Elizabeth Cady Stanton as editor, has led to its being assessed as "the least trammeled and most daring feminist paper that had yet—and perhaps has ever—appeared."[11]

Its name was apt because editor Stanton intended the weekly to "turn everything inside out, upside down, wrong side before."[12] Despite its zesty style, an international array of female correspondents, and a nose for news, the *Revolution's* circulation never reached more than 3,000, and its operating deficit increased monthly. In January 1870 the appearance of the *Woman's Journal*, a women's rights paper representing a more moderate, and consequently more popular, wing of the women's rights movement, further weakened the *Revolution's* subscription list. In May 1870 after two and a half years of publication, Stanton and Anthony severed their connection with the paper.[13]

Although the *Revolution's* publication history was tumultuous, it inspired others. In March 1869 Mary Rice Livermore founded the *Agitator* in Chicago.[14] Livermore intended to make the Midwest's first women's rights paper the "twin sister" of the *Revolution*.[15] However, aware that the outspoken New York counterpart engendered controversy, Livermore judiciously editorialized that she would discuss all aspects of the "woman question" without assailing Christianity or the "sacredness of the home and family."[16]

A moderate stance on women's rights issues and its location in the thriving Midwest contributed to the *Agitator's* success. Bloomer, former editor of the *Lily* and a resident of Iowa, attested: "I find I cannot do without the *Agitator*. The *Revolution* is a good paper and doing good work, but we of the West need a home paper, to post us on the doings of Western women, and the progress of woman's cause in the West."[17]

Despite such testimonials, the *Agitator* ceased publication after only nine months. Neither poor finances nor lack of circulation caused its demise. The paper's popularity as well as her moderate views made Livermore the logical choice to become editor of the *Woman's Journal*, the *Revolution's* rival.

Although the *Agitator* proclaimed itself a western paper, its Chicago location and the fact that it included little material from states and territories west of the Rocky Mountains, ranks it as a midwestern women's rights periodical. The claim to being the West's first women's rights periodical belonged to the *Pioneer* published in San Francisco.[18] In January 1869 Emily A. Pitts purchased a half interest in the *California Weekly Mercury*, a family paper. Ten months later, she transformed the staid publication into the *Pioneer*, named for "one who goes before with pick in hand to prepare the way for others to follow" and announced that the weekly would be "earnestly devoted to woman, her elevation and enfranchisement."[19]

After altering the paper's name, audience, and tone, the editor married August K. Stevens and from then on referred to herself as Emily Pitts Stevens. In 1873 Pitts Stevens abruptly terminated her connection with the *Pioneer*. Another woman, C.C. Calhoun, became editor and vowed to continue the paper's support of women's rights issues. However, the *Pioneer* ceased publication soon after the editorial upheaval.[20]

The *Pioneer* was instrumental in the establishment of other women's rights titles. For several months in 1871, Abigail Scott Duniway worked as the *Pioneer's* Oregon editor.[21] Duniway credited Pitts Stevens and the *Pioneer* as inspirations for her own women's rights paper, the *New Northwest*. Between 1871 and

1887 Duniway published her weekly in Portland, Oregon, making it the longest running western women's rights periodical.

The *New Northwest's* masthead proclaimed that it was "not a woman's rights, but a human rights organ." However, in an introductory column Duniway was more forthcoming about the paper's intent. She wrote:

We started out in business with strong prejudices against 'strong minded women'. Experience and common sense have conquered those prejudices. We see, under the existing customs of society, one half of the women overtaxed and underpaid; hopeless, yet struggling toilers in the world's drudgery; while the other half are frivolous, idle and expensive. Both of these conditions of society are wrong. Both have resulted from woman's lack of political and consequent pecuniary and moral responsibility. To prove this, and to elevate woman, that thereby herself and son and brother man may be benefited and the world made better, purer and happier, is the aim of this publication.[22]

The paper was the catalyst for the women's rights movement in the Pacific Northwest. However, in January 1887, Duniway's age and increased lecture responsibilities caused her to sell the paper to a Portland businessman, Oliver Mason. Although Duniway promised to continue submitting columns, in February 1887 a brusque statement announced that her connection with the paper had ended, and by March 1888 the *New Northwest* ceased publication.[23]

Like Duniway, Caroline Nichols Churchill gained her journalism experience from work on the *Pioneer*. After serving as editor/business manager of the San Francisco paper, Churchill founded the *Queen Bee* in Denver, Colorado, in 1882.[24] Another Colorado paper characterized the early issues of the *Queen Bee* "as bright and spicy and saucy as a 16 year old girl at boarding school."[25] Readers responded to the paper eagerly, and by 1883 Churchill boasted that her paper had the "largest circulation of any weekly paper published between Kansas City and San Francisco."[26]

The paper reflected its outspoken and highly opinionated editor, and thrived for thirteen years. In September 1885 a cryptic announcement told readers that the *Queen Bee* "would shut down for several weeks because of repairs and a "different arrangement." It never resumed publication, most likely because of a shortage of funds, a problem endemic to most of the women's rights periodicals.

Inspired by a growing interest in women's rights and desire to regionalize women's news, two other titles began publication. The *Woman's Chronicle* appeared in Little Rock, Arkansas, and was the South's only women's rights paper. The fact that the paper was published in Little Rock rather than in a larger city such as Richmond or Atlanta is not surprising. Located in the western part of the South, Little Rock was remote from the traditional and proscribed sex roles of the region and its women's rights activities were less restricted. Catherine Campbell Cunningham was the president of the Little Rock suffrage association and founder and editor of the *Woman's Chronicle*. Cunningham taught public school in Little Rock to support herself and her paper, which appeared for five years until illness forced her to stop publication. Her obituary commented that during its publication, the *Woman's Chronicle* "never declared a dividend, never received a donation, never owed a dollar and never missed an issue."[27]

The *Woman's Tribune* was a contemporary of the *Woman's Chronicle*. Clara Bewick Colby founded the paper in Beatrice, Nebraska, in 1883.[28] Initially financed by the Nebraska Woman Suffrage Association to serve as its official organ, the paper under Colby covered the spectrum of women's rights issues. An early editorial affirmed that the weekly would be "devoted not only to woman's political interests but to her interests in all fields of labor and thought."[29] Colby's formula was successful and within five years the paper enjoyed a weekly circulation of 7,000.[30] After relocations to Washington, D.C., in 1889 and to Portland, Oregon, in 1904, the paper lost momentum and consistency, and it ceased operation in 1909.

None of the women's rights titles were able to approach the longevity, the quality, the circulation, and the impact of the *Woman's Journal*. The stories of the paper and its founder and editor, Lucy Stone are inseparable.[31] Stone, an early activist for women's rights, was at the center of a schism in the movement during the years following the Civil War. The split focused on tactics and policies concerning the woman suffrage amendment to the Constitution. Led by Elizabeth Cady Stanton and her paper the

Revolution, the National Woman Suffrage Association (NWSA) advocated radical social changes. In 1869 Stone and her husband, Henry Blackwell, founded a joint stock company to finance the establishment of a women's rights periodical called the *Woman's Journal*, which would be the voice of the more moderate American Woman Suffrage Association (AWSA).

The first issue of the *Woman's Journal* appeared in Boston on New Year's Day, 1870, two years after the inaugural issue of rival Stanton and Anthony's *Revolution*. The *Woman's Journal* was an immediate success and all 5,000 copies sold out within three days.[32] By 1883 the paper announced that it had "perhaps 30,000 readers and is self-supporting."[33] Its editorial board and contributors were illustrious. Livermore, who had been editor of Chicago's *Agitator*, was editor-in-chief from 1870 to 1872; Julia Ward Howe was an associate editor and a long-time contributor, as was Thomas Wentworth Higginson, an early male supporter of the women's movement. Respected public figures such as William Lloyd Garrison, Louisa May Alcott, Antoinette Brown Blackwell, and Charlotte Perkins Gilman also wrote frequently for the paper.[34]

Despite its preeminence in the field of women's rights publications and its 1890 adoption as the official voice of the National American Woman Suffrage Association (NAWSA), the newly unified woman suffrage group, the *Woman's Journal* was not immune to setbacks. A 1913 article announced that the periodical had financial difficulties and might cease publication.[35] In 1917 NAWSA purchased the *Woman's Journal*, consolidated it with two suffrage papers, the *Woman Voter* and the *Headquarters Newsletter*, and named the merged papers the *Woman Citizen*. The lead editorial in the first issue of the *Woman Citizen* promised "to reflect woman as the world was beginning to know her, that is, as producer, wage-earner and citizen, as well as homemaker."[36] Until it ceased publication in 1932, after reverting to its original name in 1928, the *Woman's Journal* continued to fulfill the goal of all women's rights papers—to inform women about their rights, activities, to inspire them to assume an equal place in society.

This capsule history of eleven women's rights periodicals reflects the diversity, mixed aims, and complexity of the movement itself. The women's rights press was not a monolithic entity of cloned publications espousing the same message. Rather, it was an amalgam of periodicals, each having distinctive traits and beliefs about what equal rights for women meant. Whereas all of the women's rights titles adopted a tabloid format and appeared on newsprint, the quality of each paper and its printing varied. Some, like the *Queen Bee*, were only four pages long; others were more extensive. The *Woman's Journal* began as an eight-page weekly and later expanded to twenty-four pages. The *Woman's Journal* was the longest-lived of all the titles and ran for sixty-two years, and the *Woman's Tribune* appeared twenty-six years. Taking the other extreme in terms of longevity was the *Agitator*, which published only nine months, and the *Una*, which lasted little more than two years.

Most of the women's rights periodicals suffered from financial problems because they were so heavily dependent upon subscriptions, renewals, and advertisements, highly unreliable sources of income for fledgling reform publications. The periodicals ran frequent appeals for readers to pay for their subscriptions and to promote the publication among their friends.

Some of the periodicals, such as the *Una*, the *Revolution*, the *Woman's Journal*, and the *Woman's Tribune*, had large staffs of correspondents located across America and abroad. Others, such as the *Lily*, the *New Northwest*, the *Queen Bee*, and the *Woman's Chronicle*, were written and produced by lone editors who relied heavily upon reprinted articles from other publications.

The audiences for these periodicals were as varied as the papers themselves. The *Una* appealed to middle-class intellectuals; the *Lily* had a strong temperance following; and both the *Woman's Advocate* and the *Pioneer* attracted working women. All of them blended news of women's rights with columns on fashion, household hints, national and local news items, fiction, and poetry. Some of the periodicals adopted a radical tone such as the *Revolution*, which advocated legalized prostitution and easy divorce, and the *Queen Bee*, which offered its readers material on rape, celibacy, and birth control. Others adopted a more conservative style such as the *Lily*, the *Woman's Journal*, and the *Woman's Chronicle*.

Despite the catalog of differences, women's rights periodicals shared common characteristics. Dedicated women established the papers because the general circulation press was not providing balanced coverage of news on women and their rights. Founded to publicize and enlarge women's sphere, all of the women's rights periodicals conscientiously printed material on women's accomplishments, potentialities, and rights. All promoted women's equality, although some stressed the woman suffrage issue more than others.

An extensive network of connections existed among the papers. Very often women gained valuable first-hand journalism experience by working on sister publications. Not only did they acquire the skills to refine and improve upon their predecessors, they also gained confidence and experience to strike out and form their own women's rights paper. Bloomer worked for two temperance newspapers before assuming the editorship of the *Lily*. After serving as a contributor to both the *Lily* and the *Una*, Stanton went on to found the *Revolution*. After the *Una* ceased publication, editor Davis extended her journalism career by serving as Stanton's associate editor for a brief time. Having worked as the associate editor of her husband's Universalist monthly, Livermore gained experience to found and edit the *Agitator*, then to become editor-in-chief of the *Woman's Journal*. After a few months as the Oregon editor of San Francisco's *Pioneer*, Duniway started the *New Northwest* in Oregon. Another *Pioneer* alumna was Churchill who went on to establish Denver's *Queen Bee*.

Women's rights periodicals were significant forces in the movement to expand the role and rights of women. They provided women with a forum in their struggle for equality. Equal participation of women in all areas of life was the goal of all the papers. The means to that end was the creation of free and independent women whose minds were developed to their fullest capacities. Because of this belief, women's higher education was a prominent theme. In the editorial in which Amelia Bloomer first publicly declared her women's rights sentiments, she chose the topic of education for women. Contending that education was vital to women's lives, she wrote: "It is not our right to hold office or to rule our country, that we would now advocate. Much, very much, must be done to elevate and improve the character and minds of our sex, before we are capable of ruling our own households, as we ought, to say nothing of holding in our hands the reins of government."[37] Following her call "to improve the minds of their sex," women's rights periodicals linked women's rights and women's higher education for more than seven decades. The papers valued education for women because they deemed it to be the stepping-stone to women's equality.

NOTES

1. D.C. Bloomer, *Life and Writings of Amelia Bloomer* (Boston: Arena Press, 1895; reprint ed., New York: Schocken Books, 1975), 41. For additional biographical information on Bloomer, see W. David Lewis, "Amelia Jencks Bloomer," in *Notable American Women*, Edward T. James, and Janet Wilson, eds. (Cambridge, Mass.: Belknap Press, 1971), 1:179–181; and Louise Noun, "Amelia Bloomer: a Biography," Parts 1, 2. *Annals of Iowa* 47 (Winter, Spring 1985): 575–617, 575–621.

2. Although Jane Swisshelm founded and edited the *Pittsburgh Saturday Visiter* (1848–1857) and the paper displayed strong women's rights sentiments, it is classified as an antislavery journal. For an account of early women's reform journals, see Bertha Sterns, "Reform Periodicals and Female Reformers 1830–1860," *American Historical Review* 37 (July 1932): 678–699.

3. Bloomer, *Life and Writings*, 156. In 1860 the average circulation of a monthly magazine was 12,000 per issue, and weeklies circulated an average of 2,400 copies, according to Frank Luther Mott, *A History of American Magazines*, 5 vols. (Cambridge: Harvard University Press, 1938–1968), 2:10.

4. Louis Fox, "Pioneer Women's Rights Magazine," *New York Quarterly* 42 (January 1958): 71–74.

5. Alice Felt Tyler, "Paulina Kellogg Wright Davis," in *Notable American Women* 1:444–445.

6. *Una*, February 1, 1853, 4.

7. *Lily*, April 15, 1856, 2.

8. Eleanor Flexner and Claire E. Fox, "Anne Elizabeth McDowell," in *Notable American Women* 2:460–461.

9. *Una*, January 1855, 14.

10. *Una*, March 1855, 32.

11. Ellen DuBois, *Feminism and Suffrage: the Emergence of an Independent Women's Movement in America, 1848–1869* (Ithaca: Cornell University Press, 1978): 104. For biographical information on Stanton and Anthony and their association with the *Revolution*, see Elisabeth Griffith, *In Her*

Own Right: the Life of Elizabeth Cady Stanton (New York: Oxford University Press, 1984) and Kathleen Barry, *Susan B. Anthony: a Biography of a Singular Feminist* (New York: New York University Press, 1989).

12. Susan B. Anthony, Elizabeth C. Stanton, and Matilda J. Gage, *History of Woman Suffrage*, 6 vols. (New York: Fowler and Wells, 1881–1922), 2:373.

13. Laura Bullard became the new owner of the *Revolution*. She had been one of the paper's literary contributors and was providentially the heiress to a large fortune from the popular patent medicine, Dr. Winslow's Soothing Syrup. Under Bullard, the paper assumed a new, somewhat ironic motto, "What God hath joined together, let no man put assunder." Fashion, recipes, and hints on child-rearing filled its pages, and eighteen months after Bullard bought the *Revolution*, it lost its name and identity when the New York *Christian Enquirer* purchased it. For a full account of the *Revolutions's* history, see Lynne Masel-Walters, "Their Rights and Nothing More: A History of the *Revolution*, 1868–70," *Journalism Quarterly* 53 (Summer 1976):242-251.

14. Robert E. Riegel, "Mary Ashton Rice Livermore," in *Notable American Women* 2:410–413; and Mary Livermore, *The Story of My Life in the Sunshine and Shadow of Seventy Years* (Hartford, Conn.: A.D. Worthington & Company, 1899).

15. Anthony, Stanton, and Gage, *History of Woman Suffrage*, 2:373.

16. *Agitator*, March 13, 1869, 4.

17. *Agitator*, October 23, 1869, 3.

18. Sherilyn Cox Bennion, "The *Pioneer*: the First Voice For Women's Suffrage in the West," *Pacific Historian* 25 (Winter 1981):20–1.

19. *Pioneer*, November 13, 1869, 1.

20. For biographical material on Pitts Stevens, see Frances Willard and Mary Livermore, *American Women: Fifteen Hundred Biographies* (New York: Mast, Crowell, and Kirkpatrick, 1897), 686; and Bennion, "*Pioneer*," 19–21.

21. Ruth Barnes Moynihan, *Rebel for Rights: Abigail Scott Duniway* (New Haven: Yale University Press, 1983).

22. *New Northwest*, May 5, 1871, 2.

23. Moynihan, *Rebel*.

24. Caroline Nichols Churchill, *Active Footsteps* (Colorado Springs: Mrs. C.N. Churchill Publisher, 1909).

25. *Queen Bee*, August 19, 1882.

26. *Queen Bee*, November 28, 1883.

27. *Woman's Journal*, April 18, 1908, 63.

28. Norma Kidd Green, "Clara Dorothy Bewick Colby," in *Notable American Women* 1:355–357.

29. *Woman's Tribune,* November 1, 1883, 1.

30. *Woman's Tribune,* October 27, 1888, 3.

31. Elinor Rice Hays, *Morning Star: a Biography of Lucy Stone, 1818–1893* (New York: Harcourt Brace, 1961); Agnes Ryan, *The Torch Bearer, a Look Forward and Back at the Woman's Journal, the Organ of the Woman's Movement* (Boston: Woman's Journal and Suffrage News, 1916).

32. *Woman's Journal,* January 22, 1870, 17.

33. *Woman's Journal,* October 6, 1883, 319.

34. Two sources of information on the history of the *Woman's Journal* are Ryan, *Torchbearers,* and Lynne Masel-Walters, "A Burning Cloud by Day: The History and Content of the *Woman's Journal,*" *Journalism History* 3 (Winter 1976–1977):103–110.

35. *Woman's Journal,* December 27, 1913, 412.

36. *Woman Citizen,* June 2, 1917, 1.

37. *Lily,* October 1, 1849, 77.

2

THE PURPOSE OF
WOMEN'S EDUCATION

The ethos of the "true woman" dominated midnineteenth century society. Womanly virtues of "piety, purity, submissiveness, and domesticity" restricted women to a world circumscribed by the parlor, kitchen, and nursery. The doctrine of "separate spheres" was omnipotent, the cult of domesticity pervasive, and the subordination of women an established tradition.[1] Despite a formidable array of strictures on their minds and bodies, women were a disquieting influence upon society. The "woman question" was a constant theme of discussions as many pondered the riddle of women's nature and their appropriate role.

The awesome question "why educate women?" featured prominently in those debates. In 1853 Henry James, a prominent lecturer and social critic, proffered his response in the much-read magazine *Putnam's Monthly*. Discussing woman's right to education, James expressed a sentiment common to many when he decisively proclaimed: "Learning and wisdom do not become her." He added that woman's true nature "is not to promote the spread of science and art, is not to do battle with ignorance and superstition, is not to wrest the great field of nature from the dominion of savage beasts; it is simply to refine and elevate man."[2]

Timothy Shay Arthur, a contemporary of James and editor of a popular ladies' magazine, added his opinions to the debate on educating women. His essay "Ruling a Wife" argued that women were men's intellectual inferiors and should be submissive to the superior sex. Her publishing rival's highly publicized comments on women's intellectual frailties provoked Amelia Bloomer, editor of the *Lily*, to defend her sex. Confident in her recently assumed role as advocate of women's rights, Bloomer informed Arthur that men and women were born mental equals. However, a lack of educational opportunities and low societal esteem had eroded women's intellectual abilities. Bloomer concluded that a woman must be taught "that she was created for a higher purpose than to be a parlor ornament."[3] With that tart rejoinder, Bloomer voiced the desire of many women to be educated for a life beyond that of a decorative object.

The purpose of educating women engaged the attention of women's rights activists for future decades. Despite consensus on the necessity of education for women, women's rights papers, reflecting the opinions of the women's rights movement as a whole, gave differing answers to the question "why educate women?" Within the pages of women's rights papers, editors, writers, and readers asked themselves, "Should we be educated to be wives and mothers?", "Should we be educated for a role or job outside the home?", and less frequently, "Should we be educated for self-fulfillment?"

From 1849 to 1920 women's rights papers presented a spectrum of answers to those questions. The ever-shifting "proper" role for an educated woman colored the response. Mothers of the Republic, knowledgeable helpmates, competent citizens, financially independent workers, and trained professionals were the myriad of roles promoted, sometimes simultaneously, within the pages of the women's rights press. The diversity of opinions among women about the purpose of their education, and shifting societal pressures that influenced those opinions were evident. The women's rights press had no fixed position on an educated woman's proper role. Instead, the papers presented a variety of possibilities based on the sentiments of the editors and the influence of society.

The *Lily*'s comments on the purpose of women's education were a tentative mix of traditional and revolutionary. Its stance was ambiguous and the paper seemed reluctant to offer absolute answers because few were apparent or even imaginable. When the *Lily* began publication in 1849, women's lives consisted solely of marriage and motherhood, and female seminaries were their only source of education. Despite efforts of outstanding institutions such as Troy, Mount Holyoke, and Hartford to intellectualize women's lives, many succeeding female seminaries failed to emulate their prototypes. Most seminaries cultivated nothing more than the social graces and domestic skills of Bloomer's scorned "parlor ornament."[4]

In their efforts to improve women's education, the *Lily*, and the other antebellum women's rights papers, chose an unusual method. Instead of publishing material lauding the intellectual accomplishments of notable schools such as Troy and Mount Holyoke, the papers chose to deride the "superficial" and "frivolous" curricula and simpering students of female seminaries. In the *Lily*, editor Bloomer characterized the product of a typical female seminary as one "who has never been taught to think or to act for herself, or to have any higher purpose than to display her accomplishments and to catch a husband."[5] As a frequent contributor to the *Lily*, Elizabeth Cady Stanton addressed this issue and challenged rather than scolded. She dared young women to aspire to worthwhile accomplishments and asked "Now would it not be a more worthy ambition to see who could perform the most wonderful feats on horse or foot, who could acquire the most property, who could preach the most able sermon, or write the most popular book, who could read the best, or converse the most elegantly?"[6]

Letters from readers frequently painted an equally bleak picture about the mindless training being offered to women in many female seminaries. The *Una* printed a Georgia woman's account of the desultory pattern of female seminary education in the South, which concluded:

With the exception of a few seminaries, ephemeral boarding schools spring up here and have their existence long enough for the young ladies of our land to work a few little cats in worsted, and dogs in perforated board—or canvas, or perchance they may snatch time enough from the whirl of the dance and polka to conjugate a few Latin verbs, the impression of which only lasts till they become dissipated by the

frivolity of lighter employments. Who can deny that one of the grand
evils on the education of our sex, is a mere superficial education.[7]

By the mid-1850s criticism of the female seminaries disappeared from the papers. The "great days" of the seminaries
were past and women's rights papers turned their attention
to the more complex problem of why women should be educated. In an early issue of the *Lily*, Bloomer urged women to
"rise above the silly fashions and customs of the day, and to
educate themselves that they may realize the great purposes
of their creation."[8] As envisioned by Bloomer and many of her
contemporaries, this "great purpose" was to be that of a sensible
wife and mother. Although antebellum women's rights papers
denounced submissive, frivolous women, they did not totally
repudiate the societal vision of "true womanhood." The pervasive ideal of separate spheres influenced all women, including
editors of women's rights papers, and rendered them incapable
of envisioning a public role for women. Whereas early women's
rights editors concurred that women's education must consist
of more than frivolous accomplishments, they were ambivalent
about educated women's role outside the domestic sphere.

The ideal of the educated wife and mother was a carryover
from the days of the early republic. Women's educational needs
received serious attention because of the new country's desire for
intelligent, capable mothers to rear its future citizens.[9] Advocacy
of enlightened wives and mothers extended into the 1850s and
was a popular theme in the *Lily* and other early women's rights
periodicals.

In 1851 the *Lily* reprinted a speech by Dr. Lydia Folger
Fowler, one of America's pioneer women physicians, to the ten
female students at coeducational Central Eclectic Medical College
(Rochester, New York).[10] Fowler articulated what many women,
including those advocating women's rights, believed the purpose
of women's education to be. Speaking to young women about to
join a male-dominated profession, Fowler selected the theme of
women's education for a domestic role:

We cannot gainsay the fact that to woman is committed the care of
children, that her immediate sphere is as a queenbee in the bosom of

her family; that her strongest susceptibilities are touched when she is addressed as a mother. But this is the strongest reason why woman should awake from her mental and physical coma, why she should no longer bathe in the Lethean waters of ignorance and indolence, but be developed physically and mentally. Because woman is the mother of her children, because she has in her hands harps of 10,000 strings to tune, because she has to rear and train her offspring for time and eternity, should she hide the heaven born aspirations of her soul and be a nonentity?[11]

However, not all of the women's rights papers endorsed such sentiments. In contrast to the *Lily's* stance, the *Una* displayed no support for the concept of an educated motherhood. Editor Davis staunchly believed that women should be educated for self-fulfillment. In support of this stand, the *Una* reprinted a speech by England's Lord Palmerston in which he likened educated men to the rough stones or fabric of society while he compared educated women to the cement which gives "order, consistency and endurance." Davis acerbically disputed the British home secretary's metaphor and forcefully editorialized: "This will do for an English Lord, but we demand to be educated because we are human beings, and are accountable for the gifts given us and not because we are the appendages of man in any of our life relations, either as wife, mother or daughter."[12]

Material in the *Una* frequently railed against women's domestic role on the grounds that it limited their abilities and ambitions. A reader noted that figures from the 1850 Census of the Population reported that there were fifty-seven illiterate women for every thirty-nine illiterate men. Attributing this statistic to society's restricted view of women's abilities, she asserted:

The continual harping on 'woman's sphere'—a sphere ruled by that exalted trinity—a baby, a shirt, and a pudding, when carried out to its consequence means nothing less. For cannot a woman nurse a baby, make a shirt, or compound the abstruse ingredients of a pudding, without knowing a from zed, or a pen from a toothpick![13]

Thomas Wentworth Higginson, a Unitarian minister and an ardent supporter of women's rights, shared his opinions on the purposes of women's education with readers of the *Una*.[14] He optimistically contended that in 1853 people no longer debated whether a girl should be educated, but instead discussed what she could do with her newly attained education. Although not explicit about the proper place for the educated woman, Higginson envisioned more than a domestic role when he wrote: "Nothing can hide from me the conviction that an immortal soul needs for its sustenance something more than visiting and gardening and novel reading and crochet needles, and the occasional manufacture of a sponge cake."[15]

The *Woman's Advocate*, whose audience was working women, discussed why women should be educated more frequently than did the other women's rights papers of this era. Editor McDowell believed that women should be educated for both domestic and public roles. She contended that an educated woman would become "man's companion and friend, not his pastime nor his victim; then will be perceived the perfect harmony of their rights, the beautiful adaptation of their spheres—he the strengthening, she the refining, elevating element of their common life."[16] Despite this traditional view about the purpose of educating women, McDowell, herself an example of a woman in the public sphere, was equally sympathetic to a public role for educated women. Her readers shared similar opinions and frequently used the paper to vent their frustrations. One writer chafed at the narrowness of the traditional curriculum offered female students, as well as their eventual constricted public role. Displaying a sense of bitterness about women's lives, she wrote: "What use for her to learn to compute interest? She will never have money to loan. Why should she study philosophy? She may not apply its principles to the construction of machinery. Who would do anything so *unwomanly*?"[17] Upholding those sentiments, McDowell editorialized that both sexes should study the same subjects on the grounds that "there is no knowledge which is necessary or proper for a man, which is not equally proper and necessary for a woman."[18]

Like other women's rights activists of the era, McDowell enlisted the words of men to bolster her ideas. Advocating a strong curriculum for women, McDowell reprinted a sympathetic lecture given by Gardiner Spring, a well-known New York Presbyterian minister. Spring urged parents to instruct their daughters in more than "domestic philosophy" and to expose them to subjects such as classical knowledge, history, biology, reasoning, and thinking skills. His conclusion that "the greater variety of intellectual accomplishments she possesses, the more respectable she will become, and the more influence will she exert in any sphere which she is destined to occupy" matched McDowell's dual support of women's activity in both the home and in the world outside it.[19]

Evident in this first generation of women's rights periodicals was a difference of opinions on why women should be educated. The *Lily* advocated a traditional stance and supported women's education for responsible motherhood. The *Una* scorned that advice and emphasized the personal and intellectual benefits of educating young women. The *Woman's Advocate* publicized the somewhat radical, double-sided message that some women could be educated to be better wives and mothers, whereas others might use their schooling to secure a role outside the home. McDowell's paper even went so far as to suggest the possibility of a career, with its attendant boon of financial independence. The diversity of ideas about the purpose of women's education evident in the antebellum women's rights periodicals continued in the pages of their successors.

The Civil War inexorably reshaped society and its attitudes about women. Over a half a million men died in the four-year battle.[20] The enormous number of casualties in both sections of the country created a generation of widows, spinsters, wives with disabled husbands, and consequently expanded the pool of women in need of paid employment. After the war, self-support became a problem for many women, married and unmarried. Although the idea of separate spheres remained entrenched, its previously impenetrable facade began to show fissures.

Women's rights periodicals published after the Civil War reflected the interests of women who, by choice or necessity, were experiencing a life beyond the home. The women described and celebrated in the papers were "strong-minded." The more radical women's rights papers unabashedly campaigned for women to be educated for careers and self-sufficiency.

True to its iconoclastic reputation, the *Revolution* vehemently rejected the notion of educating women solely for domesticity and the perpetuation of separate spheres. In a forceful editorial, editor Stanton deplored the fact that young women were destined only to be "fed, clothed, guided and controlled today by father or brother, tomorrow by husband or son, never to know the freedom and dignity that one secures in self dependency and self support. . . . Multitudes of our noblest girls are perishing for something to do. The hope of marriage, all we offer girls, is not enough to feed an immortal mind."[21]

Buoyed by women's war-time accomplishments, the *Revolution* diligently promoted women's education for careers. In announcing the opening of Howard University (Washington, D.C.), an institution that accepted students regardless of race or sex, the *Revolution* urged women to attend the school "with a purpose to become proficient in business, and to win to themselves honor and independence."[22] When a woman student at St. Lawrence University (Canton, New York) wrote seeking vocational guidance, Susan B. Anthony responded with a rare self-written piece. Anthony pragmatically advised the study of theology or medicine on the grounds that "there is great demand for women in both of those fields." To further encourage the choice of a medical career, Anthony noted that a woman doctor, Clemence Lozier, earned over $15,000 a year, a lavish salary at a time when the average male earned $780 a year.[23]

Chicago's *Agitator* also stressed the connection between careers and financial independence for women. A letter from a woman doctor in Indiana spared no words on the subject and dramatically urged: "Therefore I say to every woman, not otherwise provided for—LEARN A TRADE! Study some profession! Engage in some useful occupation that will make you self-supporting, long established custom to the contrary."[24]

The West's first women's rights paper was equally forthright in its opinions of why women should be educated and the importance of being self-supporting. Editor Pitts Stevens of San Francisco's *Pioneer* criticized parents who fostered the idea that it was "vulgar and unladylike" for women to work and chastised their daughters for being "costly ornaments requiring constant care and carrying."[25] Pitts Stevens insisted that women be trained for a skill or useful purpose and reprinted an article written by "Mme. Demorest," the pen name of Ellen Louise Demorest, editor of the popular _Demorest's Monthly Magazine_. The "Mme." urged parents to teach their daughters some "remunerative business" whether they liked it or not so that the young women would be prepared for a "congenial business or profession."[26] The reprint indicated that occasionally even ladies' magazines offered women untraditional advice.

Another western paper, the _New Northwest_ of Portland, Oregon, advocated that women's education should prepare them for work or a career but acknowledged that most women would be wives and mothers. In one of her typical pieces, editor Duniway glowingly portrayed the typical woman of the period as happy in her domestic world, an equal companion to her husband, and a wise mother to her children, at the same time supporting the expansion of that limited sphere. Duniway editorialized:

We desire that she be educated for some trade or profession; that she use the natural endowment of her brain in some remunerative avocation . . . that she fit herself to live independently of man, if need be, by his side if so inclined; and in no way should she allow herself to become a clog or a hindrance to her husband.[27]

Although Duniway recognized societal pressures restricting women to the home, she was often contemptuous of women who lacked a trade or occupation and frequently labeled them "clinging vines." In a similar mode she mocked the "vine and oak" metaphor used to describe the ideal relationship between the sexes. She acerbically commented: "We go in for making the vine more self supporting, and taking some of the conceit out of the oak."[28]

Despite Duniway's strong feelings about women being educated for self-sufficiency, she published without comment an address by the female dean of the Woman's College of Willamette (Oregon) University. In four columns of florid prose, the dean detailed how her institution assisted its young women students to develop the habits and manners of "true gentlewomen." Her address made no mention of courses to cultivate their intellect or prepare them for careers.[29] It was unlike Duniway to let such a piece of "true woman" propaganda appear without her sharp editorial retorts about the need to cultivate women's brains and talents for self-support. The appearance of the piece indicates the continuing ambivalence among some women's rights activists about the proper role for educated women.

Caroline Churchill, editor of Denver's *Queen Bee*, displayed no such uncertainty. Intolerant of the cult of domesticity and the dependency of women, Churchill was an independent career woman who announced that the role should be open to all women. Commenting that a frequent theme of contemporary poetry was woman as an angel sacrificing her days and nights for the comfort of her family, Churchill wrote: "Has matrimony and maternity so little to recommend it in itself that it must be maintained at the sacrifice of every other thing dear to the soul of an ambitious woman? Ambition in woman is there for a purpose, the same as the maternal instinct, and if the former predominates, it is as much deserving of praise and respect as if it occurred in the other sex."[30]

A piece titled "Girls, Have a Purpose" warned young women that when matrimony became their sole ambition, they limited themselves to "mediocre" positions as shop girls or teachers. Noting that men with their broader aspirations advanced to more prestigious careers and better salaries, the article concluded: "Choose some course of calling and master it in all its details, sleep by it, swear by it, work for it, and if marriage crown you, it can but add new glory to your labor."[31]

Marriage and money advice often appeared together in the same articles. Churchill explained that she included numerous articles on the "pecuniary independence of women" because she did not want women to be forced into loveless marriages solely for financial security. In an unexpectedly conciliatory tone she added: "It does not mean that all women shall work in the trades and professions for their bread, or that homes shall be broken up and our sex cease to be housekeepers. It only means that for such women as are obliged to earn their daily bread there shall be the fullest, freest opportunity."[32]

The *Woman's Journal,* the most popular of the women's rights periodicals, was conservative in its opinions about why women should be educated. Articles transmitted the message that education made women better wives and mothers. Following an 1881 article lauding England for establishing women's colleges

(Girton and Newnham) at Cambridge University, editor Stone concluded: "Whoever else may be stinted, it must not be those who are to be the mothers, and hence the teachers of the world."[33] An 1882 article authored by a woman faculty member from Vassar College displayed similar sentiments. After urging college women to study subjects such as chemistry because they simplified women's household tasks, she concluded:

The most important result of education (and no education is of real value which does not give this) is a sense of responsibility of the individual; and, I believe a woman trained to scientific habits of thought and to a due realization of the responsibilities she needs, will make an excellent mother. She will know that motherhood is the highest profession the world has to offer; highest in the knowledge it requires and widest in its influence; and she will not allow a lower profession to trespass on a higher.[34]

In 1902, twenty years later, the paper printed an article relaying much the same message, this one written by a woman professor at Randolph-Macon College for Women (Lynchburg, Virginia). In the rambling piece, the author criticized the liberal arts emphasis and intellectual rigor of Bryn Mawr College's curriculum. Deeming the course of study deficient in "knowledge of houselife," the author deplored the fact that a Bryn Mawr alumna "would hardly know enough of physiology or hygiene to regulate the physical life of a little child; hardly enough of psychological laws to train the delicate organism, the child mind; certainly not enough of the chemistry or hygiene of foods to prevent hopeless indigestion on the part of the household."[35]

Even pieces written by *Woman's Journal* staff promoted the message that the goal of women's education was maternal duties. In 1898 Mary Livermore, usually a firey champion of female equality, penned an article with the revealing title "Motherhood as Vocation." She supported noted psychologist G. Stanley Hall's statement in which he declared that motherhood was the "natural" vocation of women. Although Livermore disputed Hall's suggestion that women be educated separately from men, she concurred that a differentiation in subject matter studied by the two sexes would be useful since "woman is to hand on the torch of life, to the end of time, she must be prepared for her godlike vocation."[36]

Amid these tributes to educated women's domestic responsibilities, the paper did take notice of women's ambitions for careers, professions, and jobs. In the short story "Three Little Maids from School," which appeared in an 1887 issue of the *Woman's Journal*, a trio of freshly graduated young women discussed their plans for "self support and higher development." After rejecting the occupations of sewing instructors for orphan girls, bookkeepers, and clerks, they parted. Within a short time each of them was employed. Jeanette filled in for a sick assistant in her father's leather goods store, and after a profitable business trip during which she sold a large amount of merchandise, she became her father's assistant. Mildred became a governess, traveled to exotic countries, and wrote prizewinning books about her adventures. Lillian became a nurse and, although she earned far less than her two friends, she was content with "treasures of love and gratitude." Intended to be inspirational, the story concluded with the message: "So we take leave of them, trusting that other little maids, remembering the parable of the talents that were not 'hidden in a napkin', may go and do likewise."[37] Although the story illustrated the moderating stance of the *Woman's Journal* on the proper role for educated women, it demonstrated that the paper's support for women's role outside the home was tempered by its ideas on what was considered proper "women's work." Sanctioned occupations for women were restricted to family businesses, teaching, or nursing.

Looking beyond the interests of its predominantly middle-class readership, Alice Stone Blackwell, assistant editor of the *Woman's Journal* and Stone's daughter, wrote an editorial in 1880. Titled "Unskilled Women," Blackwell's piece urged that noncollege bound, lower class women be educated for jobs. Voicing her frustration over the large number of women who came each week to the paper's office seeking jobs but offering no skills, Blackwell proposed that parents and educators eradicate women's "incapableness" and prepare them to "bear their part earnestly and capably in the work of life." She suggested training for women in mechanical arts, business, and "skillful, intelligent housework" and concluded: "Equally valuable, and more needed even, than

Wellesley or Cornell or Smith College, or Vassar, would be first-class practical Industrial and Technical schools for girls."[38]

The *Woman's Chronicle*, published in Little Rock, Arkansas, displayed an understandably conservative stance on the purpose of women's education. The South was more reluctant than other parts of the nation to recognize women as independent thinking individuals who could play public roles. Material supporting women's education for domesticity consisted mainly of reprints, published without editorial comment, as if the editor felt obliged to print them. An example was J. Sunderland's essay "Duties and Responsibilities of Educated Women." Sunderland, a minister and the editor of the religious monthly, *The Unitarian*, warned that an educated woman could be a potential enemy to the home. However, he chose to believe that she could be the home's "best friend" because the "pantry and parlor, nursery and library alike, could benefit from her knowledge." Sunderland never mentioned the possibility of a job or career outside the home for the educated woman, although he did acknowledge her role in moral and temperance reforms.[39]

Sprinkled amid paeans to traditional roles for educated women were occasional articles supporting women's education for independence. An 1888 issue of the *Woman's Chronicle* reprinted an essay titled "Girls Who Can Make Their Own Way" from the *Forum*, a reform-minded monthly review. The essay cautioned that it was "a discredit for women to be idle, to hang helpless on the men instead of doing their own work" and suggested that if women began to earn their own living, society would be much improved.[40] Another reprint, this from *School and Home*, echoed similar sentiments on the value of self-support for women and cautioned that "it is idleness, not industry, that is looked upon with scorn."[41]

Editor Cunningham's personal feelings were mixed. In an editorial she judiciously expressed her belief that women must be educated for roles both in and out of the home. Although she acknowledged that woman had a significant role to play as mother, Cunningham assured readers that an educated woman would not neglect those duties even if she assumed a broader role in society. She concluded that "the sphere of the family is not the sole sphere either of men or women, they are not only parents, they are human beings with genius, talents, aspirations, ambitions."[42] Despite her own dual career as teacher and journalist, Cunningham was not a fervent advocate of educating women for careers. Aware of deeply entrenched southern views on women's proper place, mythical as they were, Cunningham informed women that they could aspire to a variety of roles, but she remained vague about what those roles could be.

Published in the Midwest, the *Woman's Tribune* was more forthright in its views on the purpose of women's higher education. The paper clearly favored education for self-fulfillment and careers. With lavish praise for the speaker's wisdom, the *Woman's Tribune* reprinted a major section of an 1898 address by a Catholic Bishop on women's higher education in which he proclaimed:

The primary aim, however, is not to make a good wife and mother any more than it is to make a good husband and father. The educational ideal is human perfection—perfect manhood and perfect womanhood. Given the right kind of man and woman and whatever duties are to be performed, whatever functions are to be fulfilled, will be well fulfilled. Woman's sphere lies wherever she can live nobly and do useful work.[43]

Whereas most women's rights papers focused on educating women to enhance their roles as mothers or as workers, the *Woman's Tribune* campaigned for women's education for their own intellectual satisfaction. In 1902 the *Woman's Tribune* criticized the address of the Bishop of London to female students in which he said that their first duty was to the home and that they should strive to become intellectual companions to their husbands and educated mothers to their sons. The *Woman's Tribune* commented: "This is all very well and sounds very familiar, and it is in a measure true. Yet, how refreshing it would be if the Bishop had told them their first duty was to make themselves harmoniously developed human beings that might be fit for any position and duty."[44]

Women's rights periodicals confronted their readers with a variety of responses to the question "why educate women?" Educated women could be competent wives and mothers, intellectuals, or self-sufficient workers. The messages were ambivalent and illustrated that even the most articulate and outspoken writers and thinkers of the women's rights movement could not resolve the problem of what role educated women should play in society.

During the nineteenth and early twentieth centuries, women's higher education was a rapidly evolving phenomenon. Therefore it is not surprising that the purposes of women's education would be hazy and subject to change by society as well as those in the women's rights movement. The papers of the women's rights movement displayed many opinions on the subject. Although unified in their efforts to secure higher education for women and expand women's role beyond that of a "parlor ornament," women's rights periodicals suggested a variety of roles for the college-educated woman.

Society's anguish over the expansion of women's horizons beyond the mystical role of wife and mother influenced the women's rights movement and subsequently the women's rights press. Although women's rights papers were the voice of the movement to expand women's role, the papers found themselves unable to completely dissociate themselves from the strong social currents demanding education for domesticity. The women's rights press desired equality for women but found it difficult to delineate the appropriate boundaries for educated women. The forces restraining women in the home were extraordinarily powerful and difficult to flaunt.

Although many deemed women's rights periodicals to be radical in their ideas about women, most of the papers supported the idea of educating women for their domestic responsibilities. Many papers adopted a conservative stance and tempered their articles on careers for women and education for self-fulfillment with messages lauding educated women's refining influence upon the home.

Throughout their history, women's rights periodicals grappled with the issue of the purpose of women's education. For seventy-one years the papers displayed the unresolved tension between the domestic ideal and a public role for educated women. Even among women's rights proponents, the issue was a conundrum. The papers recognized a woman's multiple role as wife and mother, human being, and citizen. They gave her advice and encouragement for whichever roles she chose. Despite their ambivalent views on the purpose of women's higher education, women's rights periodicals were much-needed forums for discussions about the problem among women. The papers could not provide an answer to the question "why educate women," but for seven decades they offered a variety of options and ideas and worked to show women the options available through higher education.

NOTES

1. For overviews of women's role in nineteenth-century America, see Barbara Welter, *Dimity Convictions: the American Woman in the Nineteenth Century* (Athens: Ohio University Press, 1976); and Rosalind Rosenberg, *Beyond Separate Spheres: Intellectual Roots of Modern Feminism* (New Haven: Yale University Press, 1982).

2. Henry James, "Woman and the Woman Question," *Putnam's Monthly* 1 (March 1853): 279–286.

3. Dexter C. Bloomer, *Life and Writings of Amelia Bloomer* (Boston: Arena Press, 1895; reprint ed., New York: Schocken Books, 1975), 63.

4. Thomas Woody, *A History of Women's Education in the United States*, 2 vols. (New York: Science Press, 1929), 1: 441-456.

5. *Lily*, April 2, 1849, 29.

6. *Lily*, March 1853, 1.

7. *Una*, August 1, 1853, 103.

8. *Lily*, September 1, 1849, 71.

9. For discussions on the growth and development of the "Republican Mother" concept, see Linda Kerber, *Women of the Republic: Intellect and Ideology in Revolutionary America* (Chapel Hill: University of North Carolina Press, 1980), 189–231; and Mary Beth Norton, *Liberty's Daughters: the Revolutionary Experience of American Women, 1750–1800* (Boston: Little, Brown, 1980), 256–294.

10. Although Elizabeth Blackwell is usually credited with being America's first woman doctor, some contend that the title belongs to Lydia Folger Fowler. The basis for this contention is that Fowler, unlike Blackwell, studied at a regular medical school and held a professorship in a "legally authorized" medical school. For details on this debate, see Mary Roth Walsh, *Doctors Wanted: No Women Need Apply: Sexual Barriers in the Medical Profession, 1835–1975* (New Haven: Yale University Press, 1977), 1.

11. *Lily*, February 1852, 12.

12. *Una*, October 1853, 154.

13. *Una*, December 1853, 183.

14. Thomas Wentworth Higginson was a Renaissance man of the 1800s. Closely associated with the women's rights movement from its earliest days, he wrote for the *Una* and later was assistant editor of the *Woman's Journal* for fourteen years. For a biography of this extraordinary man, see Tilden Edelstein, *Strange Enthusiasm: a Life of Thomas Wentworth Higginson* (New Haven: Yale University Press, 1968).

15. *Una*, May 2, 1853, 57.

16. *Woman's Advocate*, February 2, 1856.

17. *Woman's Advocate*, November 10, 1855.

18. *Woman's Advocate*, June 14, 1856.

19. *Woman's Advocate*, December 22, 1855.

20. The total number of deaths in the Civil War was 618,222; 360,222 from the Union Army and 258,000 from the Confederate Army. See Bell Wiley, *The Common Soldier of the Civil War* (New York: Scribners, 1975), 117.

21. *Revolution*, June 25, 1868, 394.

22. *Revolution*, September 17, 1868, 164.

23. *Revolution*, July 23, 1868, 36. For additional information, see Milton Cantor, "Clemence Sophia Harned Lozier," in *Notable America Women*, Edward T. James, and Janet Wilson, eds. (Cambridge, Mass.: Belknap Press, 1971), 2:440–442.

24. *Agitator*, July 31, 1869, 5.

25. *Pioneer*, December 5, 1872, 2.

26. *Pioneer*, May 21, 1870, 2.

27. *New Northwest*, June 30, 1871, 2.

28. *New Northwest*, March 17, 1881, 1.

29. *New Northwest*, September 8, 1881, 1.

30. *Queen Bee*, August 9, 1882.

31. *Queen Bee*, June 6, 1888.

32. *Queen Bee*, November 9, 1882.

33. *Woman's Journal*, March 19, 1881, 92.

34. *Woman's Journal*, September 23, 1882, 298.

35. *Woman's Journal*, January 25, 1902, 26.

36. *Woman's Journal*, August 20, 1898, 268.

37. *Woman's Journal*, May 21, 1887, 166.

38. *Woman's Journal*, August 14, 1880, 260.

39. *Woman's Chronicle*, July 30, 1892, 3.

40. *Woman's Chronicle*, April 14, 1888, 5.

41. *Woman's Chronicle*, November 3, 1888, 5.

42. *Woman's Chronicle*, July 11, 1891, 3.

43. *Woman's Tribune*, January 28, 1898, 8.

44. *Woman's Tribune*, July 26, 1902, 77.

3

COEDUCATION

In 1837 the question "What should a girl do with a college education?" evolved into the more complex "Shall a girl receive the same education as a boy, in the same college, with the same instructors, and be awarded the same degree?" Oberlin College (Oberlin, Ohio) was the instigator of these disturbing concerns. In 1837 the all-male institution took the extraordinary step of permitting four women to enroll as students in its collegiate course. Four years later three of those young students, Mary Hosford, Caroline Mary Rudd, and Elizabeth Prall, became the first women to receive A.B. degrees from an American institution of higher education.[1] Coeducation introduced new complexities into debates on women's higher education and provoked concerns about the physical and mental capacities of women students as well as the future "spheres" of the two equally educated sexes.

Collegiate coeducation slumbered until after the Civil War when basic economic principles inspired the adoption of coeducation on a nationwide scale. Most states were too poor to establish two separate institutions to educate the sexes and bowed to the inevitability and financial wisdom of coeducation. In 1870, 169 or 29 percent of America's 582 colleges and universities were coeducational; by 1890 that figure had expanded to 465, or

43 percent of the country's 1,082 colleges and universities.[2]
Coeducation became an uncomfortable but inevitable fact of
higher education. In 1874 Henry Adams, editor of the *North
American Review*, remarked in his journal—perhaps with a trace
of resignation—"To resist the demand that women are making
for education is a hopeless task."[3] His comment aptly described
women's battle for coeducation. Coeducation was won neither
early nor easily. Women attained their right to joint education
of the sexes by relentlessly overcoming numerous and mercurial
blockades.

Women's rights papers viewed coeducation as a barometer of
their struggle for equality of the sexes. Their articles, letters, and
editorials provide insights into women's efforts to win equal
education and vividly show how arguments against coeducation
shifted over the decades.

Prior to the Civil War coeducation appeared primarily in
midwestern colleges, yet the early women's rights periodicals
viewed this limited adoption optimistically. In 1851 the *Lily*
reprinted a speech written by editor Bloomer for the Second
Woman's Rights Convention (Akron, Ohio). Extolling coeducation Bloomer wrote: "Men deprived of female society are inclined
to adopt coarse and vicious habits, and women deprived of male
society are not thereby improved. Bring the sexes together and
mutual benefit results—man is refined—woman is stimulated
and inspired with a higher, nobler ambition. Each sex contributes
to elevate and develop the other."[4]

Juxtaposed to Bloomer's ardor for coeducation was a disdain of
single-sex schools for women. Bloomer regarded women's schools
as inferior and uninspired in their intellectual efforts. Lavishly
praising the extensive buildings and well-qualified staff of a
newly opened female seminary in Mount Vernon, New York,
she abruptly switched the tone of her article and declared that
she wished to see the end of such institutions because "the day
of their usefulness has passed, and that the longer they continue
in existence the worse it will be for woman."[5]

Neither the *Una* nor the *Woman's Advocate* adopted Bloomer's
contempt for all-female schools. In fact, the *Woman's Advocate* reprinted a highly complimentary article from the popular weekly
Life Illustrated, which praised the buildings and curriculum of

Elmira College (Elmira, New York), a school for women chartered in 1855. At the reprint's conclusion McDowell editorialized that Elmira was "by far the most perfect institution for the education of the future women of the country that has yet been devised."[6]

Although not unified in their opinions about all-female schools, the papers were vigilant promoters of coeducation. To achieve their goal, they publicly castigated institutions reluctant to introduce coeducation. In 1854 the *Una* criticized the University of Michigan (Ann Arbor) for its refusal to enroll women students. Indignant that women were denied a place in a state institution of higher learning, editor Davis declared: "We shall continue to point to those institutions which debar us from equal rights, until their doors open, and we are asked to enter and share with our brothers, in all that is as essential for us as for him."[7] The scarcity of coeducational colleges enraged the usually serene Davis. In an 1855 editorial she noted that not more than six of the approximately 250 American colleges and universities admitted women. Davis criticized a society that "compels one half of the human family to feed intellectually on the crumbs thrown from the over-full master's hand."[8]

In addition to shaming institutions into adopting coeducation, the papers promoted its benefits to readers and reassured them of its positive effects. In an effort to ease readers' fears about the potential dangers of coeducation, editor McDowell of the *Woman's Advocate* employed homey examples. She assured women that coeducation was like growing up in a family of brothers and sisters where "each regards the other with true respect for every good quality, and gentle charity for every fault."[9]

Although coeducation was a new phenomenon, antebellum women's rights papers intuitively sensed its significance to their fight for equality. Davis of the *Una* declared that the denial of women's entrance into male colleges made "our cheeks crimson and our very fingers tingle with indignation."[10] Her sister editors expressed similar feelings and all committed their papers to coeducation's expansion.

After the Civil War coeducational institutions increased numerically and became more geographically diverse, yet women's entrance into formerly all-male bastions was not without struggle. Women's rights papers were at the forefront of the battle, promoting, cajoling, scolding, and making a public issue of women's right to equal education.

The *Revolution* was especially inventive in publicizing the multifaceted benefits of coeducation to its readers. The paper reprinted a speech in which a woman orator predicted improved marriages resulting from coeducation because "no other social relation affords so good an opportunity for knowing each other's tastes and aspirations."[11] Editor Stanton went even further and declared: "If the sexes were educated together we should have the healthy, moral, and intellectual stimulus of sex ever quickening and refining all the faculties, without the undue excitement of sense that results from the novelty in the present sense of isolation."[12]

The paper even utilized sympathetic male voices to validate its claims about the benefits of coeducation. The *Revolution* reprinted a speech by John Bascom of Williams College (Williamstown, Massachusetts), who became president of the University of Wisconsin in 1874, in which he stated:

The young lady is quicker, more enthusiastic, more intuitive in mental action. She imparts a certain brilliancy and life to the recitation room. She shames the dull indifference of the careless, phlegmatic male mind. Her lively memory and imagination and perception would enter like yeast into the heavy, torpid mass, which compose the middle and lower half of a college-class, arouse the sluggish young men to a better use of their powers, and cause a little light to find its way into their spirits. Intellectually, as well as socially, young men and young women are the complements of each other; and divorced in their training, the one class runs to froth and the other to sediment.[13]

The *Revolution* kept a close watch on institutions contemplating coeducation. Both Stanton and Anthony had been involved in the planning of the People's College, chartered in Havana, New York, in 1853. The institution proposed educating both men and women in the practical sciences, agriculture, and the classics. Although the college never opened, it became a model for the establishment of Cornell (Ithaca, New York). Because of their involvement in the People's College, Stanton and Anthony paid special attention to Cornell's coeducation plans.[14]

Despite the progressive intentions of the institution's founder, Ezra Cornell, and its sweeping motto, "I would found an institution where any person can find instruction, in any study," Cornell, established in 1868, refused to admit females until September 1872. A young woman seeking entrance to the school described her 1869 campus visit in a letter to the *Revolution*. After a tour of the buildings and a talk with Ezra Cornell, she met a number of students who, in her opinion, were "favorable and unanimous" about the admission of women. However, she discerned—quite correctly—that it was the trustees of the university who were reluctant to its becoming coeducational.[15]

The struggle for coeducation at the University of Michigan was another slow campaign detailed extensively in the pages of the *Revolution* during 1869. The paper reprinted a speech of the university's president in which he stated that his institution should be open to women, although he speculated "that few would attend."[16] In May 1869 the *Revolution* reported that Michigan's House of Representatives had passed a resolution opening the university to women students.[17] Despite the resolution, delays persisted, and it was not until January 1870 that the *Revolution* announced that Michigan would admit women. Dismissing the state's lengthy reluctance, the *Revolution* trumpeted: "Glorious Star of the North! Michigan always was a bright jewel in the coronet of republican liberty."[18]

During 1869 the *Revolution* overflowed with additional good news. Northwestern University (Evanston, Illinois), "the leading Methodist institution in the West," became coeducational.[19] An alumni committee of Brown University (Providence, Rhode Island) recommended that women be admitted to their Alma Mater.[20] At the University of Iowa (Iowa City), women made up 7 percent of the junior class, 17 percent of the sophomore class and 32 percent of the freshmen class.[21]

However, not all reports were so positive. In October 1868 the *Revolution* noted that twenty-three young women applied to Wabash College (Crawfordville, Indiana) but were rejected for admission because of their sex.[22] In the paper's next issue, one of the women refused admittance wrote an angry letter outlining the incident for the *Revolution's* readers. After describing the indignities to which the college subjected the applicants, she concluded: "They refuse to educate us, not because the laws of the college forbade, not because our moral characters were such as would contaminate those of the male students, not because we were mentally their inferiors, not because we were incapable of learning, but because God had seen fit, and most unfortunately, to create us women instead of men."[23]

As forcefully as the *Revolution* advocated coeducation, it opposed all-female schools. In a spirited piece, reminiscent of Bloomer's style, Stanton asserted: "It is the isolation of the sexes that breeds all this sickly sentimentality, these romantic reveries, these morbid appetites, the listlessness and lassitude of our girls. They need the companionship of boys to stimulate them to more active exercise and vigorous thought."[24]

Because it was the most prominent college for women at the time, Vassar College (Poughkeepsie, New York) received the observant attention of the *Revolution*. An extensive article detailed the elaborate 1869 commencement activities at which thirty-four young women received bachelor's degrees. Concluding her report of the event, the *Revolution's* correspondent declared that Vassar should be coeducational because "man without woman tends to degeneracy, like oil without alkali becomes rancid and impure—while woman alone, like alkali, inclines to evaporate and crystallize into smaller capacity."[25] Another writer described a reception sponsored by a Vassar literary society. The article criticized the college for overemphasizing dress at the expense of intellectual accomplishments. The correspondent stated: "The poor but ambitious girl will not find that college a home to her where every overdressed, brainless doll outranks talent and industry . . . We want a college to educate women, not pretty toys, and well dressed dolls, but women, who, with large heart and developed brain, will live for their sex and their country."[26]

Like the *Revolution*, Chicago's *Agitator* reported on the status of coeducation at prominent universities. Both Michigan and Wisconsin investigated the idea of establishing separate state universities for women only. Strongly opposing this alternative, the *Agitator* championed coeducation with the statement: "Not only because it is better for the sexes to be educated together, more in accordance with the natural plan, but because there is a scarcity of scholarly and trained educators to place at the head if these rapidly increasing institutions, and because the founding of another State University involves great expense and loss of time."[27]

Editor Livermore adamantly opposed women's colleges on the grounds that separate institutions for women could never be equal as long as women's inferiority to men was assumed. Using thoughtful arguments based on quality and economics, she stated:

We do not believe in colleges for women alone, any more than for men alone. It is not easy to obtain the best instruction for female colleges. The inferior position of women in our present civilization— our whole system of government being based on women's assumed inferiority—operates to keep the best educators out of the professional chairs of a woman's college. They will not accept them—or if they do, they leave to go on the faculty of the male colleges at the earliest opportunity. The best and the most of everything is provided for the male college—the female college is left to shirk for itself.[28]

The saga of nearby Wabash College's efforts to remain an all-male institution received extensive coverage from the *Agitator*. Lizzie Boyton, one of the excluded young women, wrote that the twenty-three women requested admission only to the college's recitation rooms and libraries, not to its dormitories and boarding houses. Concluding her account, she bitterly proclaimed: "Ah, you logicians of America, you who sometimes fear that suffrage is too universal, you who know that the future stability of this government depends upon the education of the masses, how dare you shut the doors of colleges against the God-appointed educators of the world?"[29]

A few months after the Wabash incident, Livermore attended a women's conference in Crawfordsville and visited the infamous institution. She delighted in commenting to her readers that the all-male institution's dormitory rooms had a "peculiar appearance" because men make "execrable housekeepers."[30]

Although the three western women's rights papers, the *Pioneer*, the *New Northwest* and the *Queen Bee*, favored coeducation, they carried few reports on it. Most western colleges and universities had been coeducational since the 1870s. Assuming that the issue had been resolved satisfactorily in their part of the country, the editors paid it little attention.

Quite the opposite was true for the *Woman's Journal*. Published in a region filled with institutions wary of coeducation, the Boston-based paper overflowed with articles on the topic. Coeducation stories dominated because Lucy Stone, the papers's founder and eventual editor-in-chief, graduated from Oberlin College, just ten years after the Ohio institution granted women their first bachelor's degrees. Convinced that coeducation was "the primary step in placing woman in her true position in society," Stone and her paper reported the countless details of coeducation's advances and setbacks.[31]

To assuage women's fears about their intellectual abilities, the paper lavished attention on the accomplishments of women students. An Iowa reader reported that at Iowa Wesleyan University (Mt. Pleasant) male students outnumbered females two to one, but the women were as academically competent as the men in belles lettres, metaphysics, and laboratory work.[32] In 1871 Moses Coit Tyler, a professor at the University of Michigan, visited the offices of the *Woman's Journal* and his heartening remarks on the first year of coeducation at his institution appeared in an article. Tyler noted that the first year's class enrolled 70 women and 1,500 men students. Women were allowed to study in all of the university's departments, the faculty were satisfied with their performance and the best Greek scholar was a woman.[33]

The reluctance of prominent institutions, such as Harvard, to adopt coeducation caused the paper much concern. In its second issue, the *Woman's Journal* tackled the issue with a front-page editorial called "Harvard Versus the 'West.'" After berating Harvard president Charles Eliot for his refusal to admit women, the editorial concluded with the soothing message: "When the thing is once done, everybody will soon forget that the practice was ever otherwise."[34] Amherst College, another all-male Massachusetts institution, was also taunted for its anticoeducational stance. In 1871 Amherst students voted to deny admission to women on the grounds that women would "lower the standards and distract men." The *Woman's Journal* ridiculed their rationale and wrote: "That the young gentlemen themselves have so little self control, are so susceptible to female attractions, and are so unaccustomed to female society, that, they, studious youths! would be reluctantly enticed from their textbooks, and debilitated in their mental tone, by the presence of bright and charming young women among them ... One cannot help wondering what sort of unfortunate experiences these Amherst students have had with young women."[35]

Even Oberlin, the vanguard institution of coeducation, was not immune to disapproval from the *Woman's Journal*. An alumna reported on events of the 1874 Oberlin commencement week for the paper. She noted that at the dedication ceremony of a new campus building, a number of students from the "early days" were on the program, but not one was a woman. A former student told the reporter that Oberlin's literary society allowed her to attend its meetings but denied her full membership and that she transferred to Boston University because of their behavior. The article concluded with the wry comment: "While Oberlin may justly claim to be one of the pioneers in coeducation, it has always striven to show that it by no means considered the sexes equal."[36]

Like other women's rights periodicals, the *Woman's Journal* was not enthusiastic about the establishment of separate women's colleges. In 1870 Stone declared: "Women's educational institutions of whatever pretensions, wherever they exist, whether legal, medical, or collegiate, hold inferior rank to those of men, and always will. . . . We did not believe in colleges for women alone, anymore than for men alone."[37] Julia Ward Howe, an associate editor of the periodical, visited all-female Vassar College and described her reactions to readers. Although impressed with the neat rooms, the delicious tea, and the "happy, wholesome" 400 students, she deplored the "dreary separation of those whom God has joined together." For Howe, coeducational institutions were "not a mutilated half world of men or women, but an integrated world of both."[38]

As more women's colleges appeared, the *Woman's Journal* subjected them to the same sharp criticism. In reporting the $2,000,000 construction cost of Smith College (Northampton, Massachusetts), Thomas Higginson bluntly stated that the money spent on elaborate buildings for the new college was an "enormous waste." He argued that it would be cheaper and better to

open Harvard to women, where all that would be needed would
be "a few boarding houses and a few additional tutors."[39] Two
years later Higginson deplored the founding of Wellesley College
(Wellesley, Massachusetts) and prophesied that: "Sooner or later,
I am persuaded, the human race will look upon these separate
collegiate institutions as most American travelers now look at the
vast monastic establishments of Southern Europe; with respect
for the pious motives of their founders, but with wonder that
such a mistake should ever have been made."[40]

By the late 1870s the *Woman's Journal's* opposition to women's
colleges mellowed, possibly because the paper recognized that
women's colleges stressed high academic standards. In 1879 Lucy
Stone, Mary Livermore, and Antoinette Brown Blackwell, self-
proclaimed "advocates of coeducation and suffrage," accepted
an invitation to visit Wellesley, which the article noted, "believes
in neither." The three skeptics spent a pleasant day at the college
and Stone described it as a place where "the cooks are men, the
professors are women." Favorably impressed with the beauty of
the campus and the liveliness of its students, Stone acquiesced:
"I am grateful to Mr. Durant (Wellesley's founder) that he has
established this institution for those whose parents are not yet
ready for the school, which like the family, does not separate the
sexes."[41]

During the 1880s articles from the *Woman's Journal* indicate that
it was a heady time for coeducation's proponents. By 1881 the
term "Harvard Annex" appeared frequently in stories describing
the plan where Harvard faculty offered a collegiate curriculum
and examinations to young women, but not a Harvard degree.
Although the concept was far removed from true coeducation,
many Harvard students regarded the Annex with apprehension.
The *Woman's Journal* reprinted an article from the student paper,
which disapproved of Annex women's use of the college library,
and their appearances in class lectures and recitation rooms. The
disgruntled student writer challenged: "If we are to have coeducation, let it be announced boldly in the catalogue and the public
press. If we are not to have coeducation, let this insidious move
in its favor be stopped."[42] In December 1882 Helen Brown, one
of the forty Annex students, shared her experiences with readers
of the *Woman's Journal*. Brown believed that Annex equipment,

books, and apparatus needed improvement, but she praised the small class size and individual attention paid to each student. Commending the Annex for its "earnest work," she hoped that it would soon receive a substantial endowment to secure its future.[43]

During the late 1880s a number of male universities and colleges, usually in the East, followed Harvard's lead and established an annex or coordinate college for women. These institutions were a compromise between coeducation and a separate college for women.[44] Although coordinate colleges alleviated the trauma of full coeducation for many tradition-bound male institutions, they infuriated women's rights activists and provoked intense discussion in the *Woman's Journal*. In 1887 the paper announced the opening of Evelyn College at Princeton University. With an acerbity previously used to describe women's colleges, the *Woman's Journal* opposed Princeton's move and vented its sentiments about coordinate colleges in general. The article declared:

Instead of the costly and clumsy method of establishing a separate college for young women in the same town, the simpler and better way would have been to open the doors of Princeton to girls. . . . It is safe to say that under the separate system the young men and women will think more about each other in a morbid way, and there will be more attempts at clandestine correspondence and flirtation, than if they met each other every day naturally and simply in the classroom, under the eye of the professors, and without the attraction of forbidden fruit.[45]

In late 1888 the *Woman's Journal* announced plans for the creation of an annex at Columbia which would provide women students with the same professors as the men students but would not establish dormitories or sleeping quarters for them.[46] Lillie Devereux Blake, president of the New York Woman Suffrage Association and author of a regular column for the *Woman's Journal* titled "Our New York Letter," called Columbia's annex "another proof of the injustice with which the 'unfortunate sex' is so generally treated."[47] Despite opposition to the annex, the *Woman's Journal* reported that twenty young women had enrolled as students in the fall of 1889. The paper commented prophetically: "In coming time, the fact that these young women could have had the advantages of Harvard and Columbia only in this way, will tell its own story of the long, hard distance up which women have had to climb to secure equal, intellectual opportunities, and it will not be to the credit of the age."[48]

The establishment of coordinate institutions was one symptom of the simmering hostility toward women college students which would come to a boil during the 1890s. Signs of the backlash against women in higher education were evident as early as the late 1880s. In 1885 the *Woman's Journal* reported that coeducational Stanford University planned to educate its men and women in separate facilities.[49] At Dickinson College (Carlisle, Pennsylvania), twenty-seven male students refused to compete in an oratory contest because a woman had entered. The *Woman's Journal* reported that she competed alone and won the gold medal while the males rang the college bell to drown her out.[50] In 1888 Adelbert College (Cleveland, Ohio), coeducational for four years, voted to no longer admit women students. The *Woman's Journal* decried that action and warned: "The conservative youth whom Adelbert wishes to attract will be attracted, while the wide awake and progressive will go elsewhere."[51]

Undeterred by the reports, the *Woman's Journal* optimistically continued to promote coeducation, announce new coeducational institutions, and applaud women's progress at older ones throughout the 1890s. The paper reported that the University of Chicago and Drexel University (Philadelphia, Pennsylvania) opened as coeducational institutions.[52] Anna Botsford Comstock, a Cornell alumna and faculty wife, authored an article proclaiming that six of the eleven newly elected members to the Cornell chapter of Phi Beta Kappa were women, ten of the twenty honors graduates were women, and a woman had won the institution's oratory prize. She commented that only small groups of faculty and students continued to oppose women and the university as a whole accepted coeducation as a matter of course.[53] In 1896 the paper reprinted excerpts from the Annual Report of the President of Tufts University (Boston), which stated that after four years of coeducation, male enrollment had not declined, interest in sports had not lessened, friction in the classroom was not evident, and women students appeared to have raised the intellectual and social tone of the school.[54]

When a report from New York State announced that women made up 56 percent of the state's collegiate enrollment during 1894, the *Woman's Journal* triumphantly proclaimed: "Utopia has come to pass in America."[55] Ironically, it was figures such as those from New York that enflamed society's fervor to restrict women's entrance to college. Many feared that women students would dominate higher education and eventually disrupt the social order.

During the 1880s college-educated women became more visible, articulate, and eager to assume prominent positions outside of the home. Society viewed this "new woman" as a threat and publicly scorned their "overeducation" and assumption of "abnormal" public roles. To squelch women's progress, a nationwide backlash against women appeared in the press, in the professions, and at coeducational colleges and universities. This backlash has been variously termed "the woman peril" or "fear of feminization" and its intent was to force women to return to private domestic roles and responsibilities.[56] The backlash was especially evident in higher education where it temporarily slowed the progress of coeducation.

By 1900 many colleges and universities attempted to restrict or bar women students. Throughout the early years of the decade, the *Woman's Journal* warily cataloged the names of coeducational institutions reverting to single-sex schools. Administrators at Colby College (Waterville, Maine) blamed a drop in male enrollment on coeducation and consequently eliminated its women's department.[57] In 1900 both Tufts (Boston) and Wesleyan (Middletown, Connecticut) limited the number of women students.[58] Nine years later, Wesleyan, coeducational since 1872, voted to return to an all-male institution. In its article reporting the decision, the *Woman's Journal* stated that students and faculty had deliberately made college life intolerable for the women students and had even gone so far as to exclude them from class day exercises.[59] A month later the *Woman's Journal* printed a letter from the president of the Wesleyan student body. He boasted that students had actively opposed coeducation for fifteen years and declared: "Our action throughout, has been one of passive ignoring. The women in college are not opposed because they are women, but because they are in college."[60]

Although the University of Chicago was not as crude as Wesleyan in its efforts to oust women, it did institute a number of restrictions on them. In 1902 the *Woman's Journal* reprinted President William Rainey Harper's assessment of ten years of coeducation at the school. Declaring himself a supporter of coeducation, Harper noted that not all of the ramifications of coeducation were yet evident. Foreshadowing future events at his institution, he concluded: "Certain limitations have already clearly fixed themselves. It is not deemed proper that men and women should take physical education together in the gym. It has never been proposed that they should occupy the same halls or dormitories. It is possible that experience will call attention to other limitations."[61] His remarks were more than speculative; six months later the *Woman's Journal* carried the headline "Coeducation Half Abolished at Chicago." The accompanying article reported that the university planned to place freshmen and sophomore men and women in separate classes and living quarters. The paper commented: "We have refrained from speaking of this matter until we were persuaded that it is a living issue, a pending change of vast significance. This is not a woman's question. The future quality and character of the education provided for boys as well as for girls is here involved." The paper went on to note that the president and the majority of the faculty had voted to abolish coeducation in the freshmen and sophomore classes. The *Woman's Journal* urged women to write letters of protest.[62]

On the West Coast, Stanford University (Palo Alto, California) instituted a quota on women students. Beginning in 1899 women were limited to 500 places in the university. The *Woman's Journal* reprinted a *San Francisco Examiner* interview with Mrs. Leland Stanford, a co-founder of the school. To explain the quota, Stanford noted that in 1888-1889 there were 480 women among the college's 1,100 students and she did not wish to see the college become a "female institution."[63]

In the 1900s headlines such as "The War on Coeducation" and "Coeducation Assailed" announced reports of new restrictions against women college students. In the midst of the furor, the *Woman's Journal* attempted to bolster morale by printing supportive articles by two important women activists from different eras. Early in 1902, just months before her death, Elizabeth Cady Stanton wrote a piece reassuring *Woman's Journal* readers that coeducation would never obliterate the differences between the sexes and should be maintained. With her usual zest, she wrote:

Scientists do not warn the florists to cease cultivating double roses lest they should turn into cabbages, or the smaller fruits lest they should turn into pumpkins. However much the rose may be increased in size, varied in color, and intensified in fragrance, it will be a rose still. The coeducation of the sexes, the study of math, abstruse sciences, and languages, medicine, and theology, and skill in the industries will have no more influence in changing girls into boys and women into men than have these improvements in vegetable life in changing the male and female elements in fruits and flowers.[64]

A few months later, the paper reprinted an address made by Carrie Chapman Catt, the newly elected president of the National American Woman Suffrage Association, to the annual meeting of the National Education Association. Catt expressed her concern over the opposition to coeducation. She speculated that such a feeling existed because many believed "in some mysterious way that men are being defrauded of the rightful prerogatives by coeducational college women" and that college-educated women were undermining the "sacredness of home and the nobility of motherhood." Like Stanton, Catt argued for coeducation. She proclaimed: "There is no sphere for men and no sphere for women, but a joint responsibility is laid upon both to give their best and highest service to the uplift of the race."[65]

The fight to preserve coeducation took place largely in the pages of the *Woman's Journal*. Although the *Woman's Tribune* and the *Woman's Chronicle* were contemporaries of the *Woman's Journal* between 1883 and 1909, it was the Boston paper that assumed the role of coeducation's champion. The southern *Woman's Chronicle* had little to say on the progress or lack of progress of coeducation in its region, most likely because the news was so dismal. Accounts in the *Woman's Tribune* surfaced mainly during the backlash years of the early twentieth century. Editor Colby, a graduate of coeducational University of Wisconsin, detailed the numerous curtailments on women students but inexplicably did not make coeducation a major issue of her paper.

After 1910, articles about coeducation virtually disappeared even from the pages of its most vigorous supporter, the *Woman's Journal*. Its editors, writers, and readers shifted their attention to the booming woman suffrage campaign. Coeducation was no longer a front-page story. It had become acceptable and taken for granted by young women contemplating a college education. In eighty years coeducation had expanded from a single Ohio institution with four women students to more than 354 colleges and universities enrolling 96,000 women students in 1920. Coeducation's staunchest supporter throughout those years was the women's rights press. The power of the press is impossible to measure and the effect of women's rights papers on coeducation's growth and institutionalization is incalculable. However, the papers' efforts to promote and foster the movement assisted many young women in their efforts to secure a college education. Women's rights papers concerned themselves with interactions between women and education and they evidenced attention to women students as well as to those on the other side of the desk—women teachers.

NOTES

1. For details about the first four women students at Oberlin, see Frances Hosford, *Father Shipherd's Magna Charta: A Century of Coeducation in Oberlin College* (Boston: Marshall Jones Co., 1937), 56–79. For discussions on the thesis that coeducation at Oberlin was implemented with masculine priorities in mind, see Ronald W. Hogeland, "Coeducation of the Sexes at Oberlin College: A Study of Social Ideas in Mid-Nineteenth-Century America," *Journal of Social History* 6 (Winter 1972–73): 160–176.

2. Mabel Newcomer, *A Century of Higher Education for American Women* (New York: Harper & Brothers, 1959), 37.

3. Henry Adams, "Dr. Clarke's 'Sex in Education'," *North American Review* 118 (January 1874): 142.

4. *Lily*, August 1851, 58.

5. *Lily*, October 16, 1854, 149.

6. *Woman's Advocate*, December 8, 1855.

7. *Una*, September 1854, 335.

8. *Una*, August 15, 1855, 121. Davis underestimated the number of coeducational colleges. Complete accuracy on names and numbers of colleges before 1870 is difficult; however, James Monroe Taylor's

Before Vassar Opened (Boston: Houghton Mifflin, 1914), 51–76 and the appendices of Annie Nathan Meyer's, *Woman's Work in America* (New York: Henry Holt, 1891) show that more than six coeducational colleges existed in 1855 when Davis wrote her article.

9. *Woman's Advocate,* June 14, 1856.

10. *Una,* September 1854, 335.

11. *Revolution,* April 8, 1868, 211.

12. *Revolution,* August 13, 1868, 81.

13. *Revolution,* November 19, 1868, 314.

14. For a discussion of the People's College and the roles of Stanton and Anthony in its development, see Charlotte Williams Conable, *Women at Cornell: the Myth of Equal Education* (Ithaca, N.Y.: Cornell University Press, 1972), 36–38; a more general account, with no mention of the influence of women on the institution, appears in Thomas Waterman, *Cornell University: A History,* 2 vols. (New York: University Publishing Society, 1905), 1:38–59.

15. *Revolution,* April 11, 1869, 197.

16. *Revolution,* March 4, 1869, 137.

17. *Revolution,* May 8, 1869, 280.

18. *Revolution,* January 20, 1870, 42.

19. *Revolution,* July 22, 1869, 39.

20. *Revolution,* September 16, 1869, 170. Despite the alumni recommendation of coeducation, Brown did not admit its first women students until 1891. In that year, Brown established the "Woman's College of Brown University," later known as Pembroke College. For an account of women students at Brown's coordinate college, see Grace Hawk, *Pembroke College in Brown University: The First Seventy-Five Years 1891–1966* (Providence: Brown University Press, 1967).

21. *Revolution,* January 21, 1869, 35–36.

22. *Revolution,* October 8, 1868, 221.

23. *Revolution,* October 15, 1868, 230–231.

24. *Revolution,* January 29, 1868, 57.

25. *Revolution,* July 1, 1869, 412.

26. *Revolution,* December 23, 1869, 389.

27. *Agitator,* May 1, 1869, 5.

28. *Agitator,* May 8, 1869, 4.

29. *Agitator,* March 20, 1869, 1.

30. *Agitator,* October 2, 1869, 4.

31. *Woman's Journal,* July 20, 1872, 229.

32. *Woman's Journal,* March 19, 1870, 82.

33. *Woman's Journal,* December 9, 1871, 388.

34. *Woman's Journal,* January 8, 1870, 1.

35. *Woman's Journal*, October 28, 1871, 346.

36. *Woman's Journal*, September 19, 1874, 300.

37. *Woman's Journal*, July 16, 1870, 220.

38. *Woman's Journal*, February 3, 1872, 36.

39. *Woman's Journal*, November 30, 1872, 377. For a description of the "elaborate design" of Smith College so vilified by Higginson, see Helen Lefkowitz Horowitz, *Alma Mater: Design and Experiences in the Women's Colleges From Their Nineteenth Century Beginnings to the 1930s* (New York: Knopf, 1984), 69–81.

40. *Woman's Journal*, November 28, 1874, 378. For a description of Wellesley College and its early building plans, see Horowitz, *Alma Mater*, 42–55.

41. *Woman's Journal*, July 5, 1879, 212. For a lively account of the development of Wellesley College and its all-female student body and faculty, see Patricia Palmieri, "In Adamless Eden: A Social Portrait of the Academic Community at Wellesly College, 1875–1920," Ed.D.diss., Harvard University, 1981.

42. *Woman's Journal*, January 15, 1881, 22. For a full account of early coeducation at Harvard and the eventual establishment of Radcliffe College, see Sally Schwager, " 'Harvard Women': A History of the Founding of Radcliffe College," Ed.D. diss., Harvard University, 1981.

43. *Woman's Journal*, December 2, 1882, 383.

44. Thomas Woody, *A History of Women's Education in the United States*, 2 vols. (New York: Science Press, 1929), 2:304–320.

45. *Woman's Journal*, January 29, 1887, 34. Evelyn College, Princeton's coordinate college, lasted only ten years and graduated fifteen young women. For information on Princeton's early ventures in educating women, see Adelaide Sterling, "Evelyn College," *Harper's Bazaar* 29 (September 1896): 806–807; and Patricia Graham, *Community and Class in America* (New York: John Wiley & Sons, 1974), 194–197.

46. The Annex, later named Barnard College, opened in September 1889 and admitted thirty-six women to its first class. See Horowitz, *Alma Mater*, 134–142.

47. *Woman's Journal*, December 1, 1888, 383.

48. *Woman's Journal*, October 12, 1889, 321.

49. *Woman's Journal*, November 28, 1885, 377.

50. *Woman's Journal*, July 17, 1886, 225.

51. *Woman's Journal*, February 4, 1888, 35.

52. *Woman's Journal*, December 26, 1891, 447; January 17, 1891, 24.

53. *Woman's Journal*, July 14, 1894, 218.

54. *Woman's Journal*, January 30, 1897, 35. Despite its glowing 1896 report, in 1900 Tufts limited the number of women students, and in

1907 the school experienced severe financial problems, which it blamed on coeducation. To remedy the fiscal situation, in 1910 Tufts established a coordinate college for women, Jackson College, and reverted to being a single-sex school.

55. *Woman's Journal*, July 14, 1894, 220.

56. For an analysis on the backlash movement that figured so prominently in women's lives during the 1890s and 1900s, see Peter Filene, *Him/Her/Self: Sex Roles in Modern America*, 2nd ed. (Baltimore: Johns Hopkins University Press, 1986), 69–83; and Rosalind Rosenberg, *Beyond Separate Spheres: Intellectual Roots of Modern Feminism*, (New Haven: Yale University Press, 1982).

57. *Woman's Journal*, March 30, 1901, 98.

58. *Woman's Journal*, October 6, 1900, 316.

59. *Woman's Journal*, March 6, 1909, 38.

60. *Woman's Journal*, April 10, 1909, 58.

61. *Woman's Journal*, January 11, 1902, 24.

62. *Woman's Journal*, June 21, 1902, 196. The University of Chicago's move to segregate women caused a nationwide storm of controversy. In 1902 separate classes for freshmen and sophomore women were instituted, but within five years the policy collapsed because of expense and bureaucracy. The threat to coeducation at the university has been described in Rosenberg, *Beyond Separate Spheres*, 44–53; and Barbara Solomon, *In the Company of Educated Women* (New Haven: Yale University Press, 1985), 56–58.

63. *Woman's Journal*, June 24, 1899, 194. For a clear account of Stanford's "five hundred limit" written by the college's registrar at the time, see Orin Elliott, *Stanford University: the First Twenty-Five Years* (Stanford: Stanford University Press, 1937), 132–136. In 1904 Stanford graduates agreed to another restriction—a ratio of three males to every female. This ratio was in effect until 1933; see Solomon, *Company of Educated Women*, 59.

64. *Woman's Journal*, February 1, 1902, 38.

65. *Woman's Journal*, July 26, 1902, 234-235.

4

WOMEN AS TEACHERS

Prior to 1830 the teacher in the village schools that dotted America was most often a man. Although teaching began as a male profession, it quickly accepted women into its ranks. The ever-expanding common school system demanded large numbers of teachers, and women became a major source of supply.

By 1846 Horace Mann, the best-known educator of the era, validated women's entrance into the profession by publicly stating: "It is found that females will teach young children better than males, will govern them with less resort to physical appliances, and will exert a more genial and kindly, a more humanizing and refining influence upon their dispositions and manners."[1] Other national figures such as DeWitt Clinton, Henry Barnard, Thomas Gallaudet, Emma Willard, and Catharine Beecher added their voices to the call for women teachers. By far, Sarah Hale was the most influential force. The indomitable editor of *Godey's Lady's Book*, Hale defined "woman's sphere" in the pages of her extraordinarily popular magazine. She viewed teaching as a natural extension of woman's role as guardian of the young. Promoting it as an eminently suitable vocation for women, she gushed that teaching was "wide enough for the display of all their genius, and there are laurels sufficient to satisfy the most ambitious."[2]

Approval by Hale and other prominent figures was a powerful inducement and teaching quickly became women's "true profession." Between 1834 and 1850 the number of women teachers employed in Massachusetts swelled from 3,000 to 5,500, a gain of more than 80 percent.[3] Figures from the 1880 *Report of the Commissioner of Education* showed a similar national pattern: California employed 2,387 female teachers and 1,208 males; Kansas 4,274 females and 3,506 males; and Ohio 12,358 females and 11,326 males. In 1880, just thirty years after their entrance into teaching, women had become 57.2 percent of the profession.[4]

Although teaching extended the perimeters of woman's sphere and provided women with a salary and meaningful occupation, women's rights papers were less sanguine about women's role in teaching than was Sarah Hale. Editors of women's rights papers viewed teaching with skepticism and scorn gained from first-hand experience. Eight of the eleven editors had been teachers themselves and had personal knowledge of women's role in the profession.[5] The papers informed readers that women would never be totally accepted in their "true profession" and were doomed to subordination to men in terms of wages, promotions, and professional recognition.

The poor wages paid to women teachers was a dominant story in women's rights papers from the *Lily* to the *Woman Citizen*. A major factor in the ready acceptance to employ women teachers was their willingness to work for lower wages than their male counterparts. Women teachers were told that theirs was a noble profession and they would be rewarded by spiritual and patriotic recompense rather than by large sums of money. This was a commonly accepted fact of employment and an Ohio superintendent of common schools boasted in his annual report that areas employing female teachers were "able to do twice as much with the same money as is done in those counties where female teachers are almost excluded. As the business of teaching is made more respectable, more females engage in it, and the wages are reduced."[6] An 1855 article in the *Lily* titled "Unequal Remuneration of Woman's Labor" disputed this assumption. Documenting the universal policy of paying a woman teacher one third to one half less than a male teacher, the *Lily* labeled it a "barbarous custom."[7]

Women teachers also chafed at their lack of recognition by professional teachers' associations. When such associations were established, women had no voice, although they constituted the majority of members. In 1845 Rhode Island, New York, and Massachusetts founded the first state teachers' associations, and by 1856 fourteen more existed in states from Alabama to Wisconsin. In 1857 the National Education Association (NEA) was established. State teachers' associations and the NEA shaped the teaching profession and molded public opinion concerning education and teachers. Their meetings were centers for discussions of controversial issues and the promotion of progressive ideas. Despite their growing numbers, women played a marginal role in the activities of the professional teaching associations. Many state associations did not permit women to be members and if they were admitted, they were not allowed to lecture, to present papers at meetings, or to hold offices or committee assignments.[8] Following the lead of the state associations, the 1857 constitution of the NEA restricted its membership to "gentlemen" only.[9]

A personal account of women's lowly position in a state teachers' association appeared in a letter to the *Lily* written by Frances D. Gage, an early women's rights activist. Gage attended the first convention of the Missouri State's Teachers' Association at which 100 delegates represented more than twenty counties. She reported that although the majority of Missouri teachers were women, the convention was run "as if only men were there," women held no committee assignments and did not appear on the program.[10]

Although the *Una's* editor was not a former teacher, the paper was more outraged by women's subservient role in teaching than was the *Lily*. Readers' letters frequently commented on the unequal pay issue. A Columbus, Georgia, teacher wrote that she was searching for another job because of her poor salary. Her limited career alternatives were "making shirts" or "keeping a boarding house," and she bemoaned the fact that women were so restricted in their choice of livelihoods.[11] An anonymous writer reported that the annual report of Boston's superintendent of schools showed that "the lowest salary paid to a male teacher is twice as much as the highest paid to a female, and that the highest paid a male teacher is six times that of the highest paid female."[12]

Davis was not reluctant to express her own sentiments on the pay issue. In a letter from the editor addressed to "Dear E," (most likely Elizabeth Cady Stanton), Davis wrote that she had recently attended the final examinations of the Providence (Rhode Island) Normal School. She noted proudly that most of the pupils were young women who had passed the examinations with outstanding scholarship. Yet she was disheartened because "with all this superior ability, the young men of the same class will receive double the salaries as teachers that the most accomplished scholars among the girls can command. A male teacher receives from $50 to $75 per month, while a female can obtain only $15 or $20; and who will say that the duties of one are less arduous than the other?"[13]

Davis criticized *Godey's* Sarah Hale for her highly publicized request that the U.S. Congress establish a normal school in every state for the free education of women teachers. The *Una's* editor sagely commented: "We do not want it because it will be more economical for the state to have female teachers." Instead, Davis suggested that Hale should exert her influence to see that women receive "education and remuneration equal to that of men."[14]

In the decade between 1870 and 1880 the number of women teachers swelled from 84,548 to 153,372.[15] As their ranks increased, so did the accounts of injustices reported in the women's rights press. Pay inequities continued as the most prominent theme. Although Susan B. Anthony, the owner/business manager of the *Revolution*, had been a teacher for some years, it was editor Stanton, with no teaching experience, who wrote frequently about the pay issue. Stanton's firey editorial "The Degradation of Women" unsympathetically chastised women teachers by complaining that they outnumbered men not because they were better teachers, but because "woman, by her cheap labor, has driven man out and degraded that profession."[16] Weekly articles recounted the harsh facts of the pay discrepancies between male and female teachers. One article noted that in thirty-nine major U.S. cities, women teachers received less than two-thirds to three-quarters salary than that of their male counterparts.[17] After reporting yet another article on salary differentials, Stanton acerbically commented, "Robbery is not all committed in the night nor on the highway."[18]

Personal stories from readers were especially poignant. A Michigan woman wrote that her town employed nineteen teachers: the three men received $75 to $120 a month, the sixteen women, $30.[19] A Rochester, New York, reader noted that although the city's board of education commended women school administrators for being as competent as men, the board voted to pay women principals $500 and males $1,200 a year.[20] An Ohio reader related the story of a woman paid $40 a month to teach fifty-five students "in a small, ill-lighted, poorly ventilated room, . . . while they pay a heavy, backheaded, sensual looking, vulgar mouthed ignoramus $60 per month to teach twenty to twenty-five scholars. He has a light, airy room and everything comfortable."[21]

Along with accounts of pay discrimination came reports of the lack of promotional opportunities for women. A New York reader deplored the fact that males had been named as principal and vice principal of the city's newly established normal school. Passed over in the process was the woman principal of a female school that had been training teachers prior to the opening of the normal school. The new male principal received $4,500, whereas the combined salaries of the overlooked woman principal, her vice principal, and her first assistant teacher amounted to only $3,700.[22]

Accounts from the Midwest were similar. Editor Livermore of Chicago's *Agitator* commented: "The average salary paid to female teachers in this state (Ilinois) last year was $48–50 per month. To men, they averaged three times as much, and yet both do about the same work."[23] A male reader reported that his town employed a male graduate of the University of Vermont who was an incompetent teacher and a young woman normal school graduate who was extremely able in her teaching; however, the male was paid "as much wages for teaching that school a day as the young woman was for teaching a week."[24]

Although women's rights papers reported salary injustices, they did little to explore the underlying causes of the problem. In a rare analytical piece, editor Livermore offered some insightful comments. Like Stanton, she blamed an oversupply of women for the salary differentials because as she noted: "There are forty women applicants on the average for every vacancy in the department of teacher. The number of properly qualified men teachers is so few that they are able to dictate their own terms." Secondly, women lacked suffrage and Livermore noted that "all disenfranchised classes are subjects and dependents."[25]

To dissuade women from choosing teaching as a career, the *Agitator* reprinted a biographical sketch of an anonymous but prominent Illinois woman. Aptly titled "What a Girl Can Do," the article dramatized the message that there were better careers for women than teaching. The subject of the article was a recent Illinois Normal School alumna who left her teaching position to run her deceased father's furniture business. Noting that the woman's annual salary in her new occupation was more than $7,000, the article bluntly concluded: "Had she taken the advice of those who consider that they have settled the great question of the age, she would now be toiling in a schoolroom, worn out, jaded and wretched on a miserable salary of $40 a month. Instead of that she is free and independent and rich."[26] Although the *Agitator* discouraged women from teaching, the paper failed to print articles presenting viable alternatives. Few young women would inherit a father's store, yet the paper did not suggest alternate careers that would provide them with better pay and greater personal satisfaction.

Farther west the problems did not change. The *Pioneer* focused on women teachers in the San Francisco area. Editor Pitts Stevens editorialized that the position of deputy superintendent of San Francisco Public Schools, with its generous salary of $3,000 a year, had been awarded to a man rather than to a woman. She concluded her article with the information that San Francisco's 312 women teachers earned an average salary of $829, whereas the thirty-seven male teachers earned an average of $1,720 a year. She blamed this inequity on the fact that women lacked political influence because they were not allowed voting privileges.[27] Although suffrage was not a major theme in women's rights papers of this era, it appeared occasionally as a secondary theme in articles on equality for women.

The *Pioneer* was the first women's rights papers to report on a new form of discrimination, the dismissal of women teachers when they married.[28] In 1870 San Francisco's board of supervisors passed a resolution demanding that women teachers give up their positions when they wed, an action Pitts Stevens termed an "outrage." She asserted that married women teachers were superior to those that were single because they could "devote themselves to the work before them with more attention, earnestness, and perseverance."[29]

Like the *Pioneer*, the *New Northwest* envisioned itself as a prominent force to improve the lot of women teachers in the area. It, too, recorded discrimination against married women teachers. Editor Duniway editorialized on the matter and declared: "A married woman has the same right to seek and obtain and receive pay for work that a married *man* has. Whether her private affairs will permit her to do the work is another matter, one of which she is the best, if not the only judge."[30] Obviously the issue was controversial among women. The *New Northwest* reported that unmarried women teachers in Sacramento, California, waged a . protest against the reappointment of married women teachers because they desired "'deserving girls' to have a chance."[31]

Although Duniway's paper was frank and outspoken on many issues, it was Denver's *Queen Bee* that reported a more serious problem, the sexual harassment of women teachers. The topic was taboo among the other women's rights papers, none of which even hinted at it. Editor Churchill announced that she received four to five complaints a year from women teachers. Although Churchill stated that it was a common problem for women teachers, even her paper reported on it only once and carried no follow-up material. In the pessimistic article, she noted that if a woman teacher resisted the sexual advances of her superior she was dismissed; if she took the complaint to court, her case was treated unsympathetically.[32]

Not even a hint of such a problem appeared in the conservative *Woman's Chronicle* of Little Rock, Arkansas. However, Catherine Cunningham, editor by night and public school teacher by day, was uncharacteristically outspoken on society's treatment of her colleagues. In a front-page editorial, she asserted that after "soap and water," women teachers "were the greatest civilizers" and she blamed their low pay and status on the fact that "women were not legally equal to men."[33] Cunningham's protests about society's disregard for her colleagues were neither novel nor earthshaking, but the fact that she was a teacher in a southern town and wrote so publicly and assertively on the issue was. Clara Colby, editor of the *Woman's Tribune*, was another former teacher and the thrust of much of her paper's material was to secure more leadership positions for women educators. Articles hailing such triumphs, usually in western cities, dotted the pages. A group of teachers from Portland, Oregon, wrote to inform readers that Ella Sabin, a teacher with fourteen years in the school system, had become superintendent of schools. Her salary was $3,000 and she supervised eighty-four teachers, only six of whom were male.[34]

Lucy Stone, another editor with classroom experience, also devoted many columns to detailing the plight of women teachers. As a young woman, Stone taught school for a dollar a week, and consequently the wages of women teachers featured prominently in *Woman's Journal* articles. Because the paper had such a wide readership, reports on the pay issue came from geographically diverse areas and emphasized the universality of the problem. Even socially concerned organizations, such as the freedmen's schools of the South, took advantage of women teachers. In 1870 the paper printed a letter detailing salary injustices endured by educated northern white women while serving as volunteers in the freedmen's schools in Atlanta, Georgia. Despite their lofty intentions to educate and improve the lives of former slaves, school administrators knowingly discriminated against their female teachers. The writer, herself a teacher in one of the many freedmen's schools, described her female colleagues as "first-rate" graduates of colleges such as Oberlin and Mount Holyoke but ranked the male teachers as "second and third rate." She stated that not one woman teacher received more than $15 a month, whereas all the men received $30 and more, except for one male who assisted a woman teacher and received $20—$5 more than the woman he was assisting. Her bitter letter noted that men were consistently paid more and were given lucrative administrative positions.[35] Her charges provoked an immediate response from J.H. Chapin of the New England branch of the Freedmen's Commission. In his letter to the *Woman's Journal*, Chapin claimed that "what may be true in a single case, or in the practice of one society, is not true as a general rule." He assured the periodical that his Boston-based society made no distinction in wages between men and women teachers when they performed the same duties. However, he did admit that "there have been and are still positions which women cannot conveniently or consistently fill . . . and in such instances, men were necessarily employed, and such wages paid as were required to secure those of tact and experience."[36]

Decades later the problem persisted. In 1911 a Florida reader reported that when she and other female teachers requested equal pay with male colleagues, they received dismissal notices over the summer.[37] In 1916 a Boston teacher produced figures showing that a female teacher in Boston had to teach seven years to earn the salary a male received during his first year of teaching in that city.[38] A reader told that she and other women teachers in the Detroit school system were forced to wash dishes in their boarding houses in lieu of paying rent, take in sewing, or work weekends and evenings in neighborhood stores to earn enough money to pay basic living expenses.[39] Although women won suffrage in 1920, the problem remained. The *Woman Citizen* excerpted an N.E.A. report showing that railroad messengers and attendants received $700 a year, whereas the average teacher salary in 1918 was $630.64. The paper caustically noted that it appeared to be more important "to mind trains, than to train minds."[40]

Closely allied to discriminatory pay practices was the lack of career advancement opportunities for women educators. A Boston reader related that in her city's female grammar schools, there was only one female principal; she received $1,700, whereas the male principals of the other female schools received $3,000. When the principalship of one of those schools fell vacant, women were not permitted to apply on the grounds that the job required more "executive power" than the majority of women teachers possessed.[41]

The paper attempted to foster appointments of women school administrators by providing substantive documentation of women's ability. In 1874 it reprinted salient sections from the 37th Annual Report of the Cleveland (Ohio) Public Schools. Five years before, the Cleveland school system had appointed women principals in its smaller schools; the Annual Report announced the results of this experiment. All of the findings were positive: schools run by women showed improved general order, superior school yard deportment, more harmonious work between assistants and principals, better teaching, fewer changes in textbooks, and a "more unquestioning obedience" to the rules of the board of education.[42]

Despite the female-inspired improvements, nine years later the *Woman's Journal* reported that the Cleveland Board of Education contemplated abolishing its women principals, and the paper urged readers to organize and oppose the move.[43] The plan to remove women principals from Cleveland schools was symptomatic of the national backlash during the 1890s and early 1900s against educated women.[44] Evident in all areas of society, the backlash extended into public education where many believed that women had become too dominant in the public schools. It was a popular belief that the overly female teaching force would have a detrimental effect on students, especially males.

Opposition to women in the schools had appeared in the *Woman's Journal* from its earliest days of publication. In 1872 the periodical quoted from the Annual Report of the Manchester (New Hampshire) superintendent of schools, which admitted paying male teachers more because of their "higher and nobler work upon the character of their pupils. We trust to them mainly, in their capacity as masters and directors of large schools, for the development not only of a thorough scholarship, but of a courteous, upright and honest manhood in the youth of our schools."[45]

During the time of the backlash against women, women educators were as unpopular as educated women. In 1892 the *Woman's Journal* reported on a Chicago controversy over appointing women principals in the primary schools. Caroline Corbin, a leading antisuffragist, and her group opposed women school administrators because they posed an "emasculating threat" to the school. Corbin argued that women were not fit to teach the "future citizens to be strong, self-reliant" nor could they instill "the ways of men in their civic capacity." The *Woman's Journal* responded: "To exclude women, arbitrarily and by an unwritten law, from all the higher positions, is an injustice to women, an injury to the schools, and an object lesson in contempt for women to all pupils."[46]

After reading about the Chicago incident, a Philadelphia reader related that a similar move had occurred in her city, an example of how important the information function of the women's rights press was. The Philadelphia Board of Education ruled that women could be neither principals of grammar schools where boys were taught, nor be permitted to teach in the upper grades of such schools. The reader noted that since most of the Philadelphia schools were coeducational, the ruling excluded women from all administrative positions and upper level teaching jobs.[47]

Individuals as well as school boards found women teachers disconcerting. Such sentiments were evident in a letter to the paper from Austin Lewis of San Francisco. In an impassioned letter outlining his opposition to women teachers, Lewis argued that a young boy was a "fighting animal" and "the chief concern of modern education should be to furnish him with the equipment of a strong resourceful fighter. Later on he must fight those of the same sex as himself, and strive with them for position, and even for the means to live." Lewis continued that only through instruction by male teachers would the young boy learn "to be at home with his own sex and familiar with its point of view."[48] The editorial comment on the letter politely disagreed and stated that the most important thing in the education of any boy was a "superior teacher of either sex, who governed by force of personality rather than physical force."[49]

Women teachers came under attack not only by their own countrymen but from foreigners as well. In 1904 the Mosely Commission, a group of British academics and politicians, made a formal observation of American education. In the report concluding the visit, the Commission predicted the ruin of the United States because of the "feminization of its men" who were taught daily by an "army of women teachers."[50] In its response to the Commission's remark, the *Woman's Journal* commented tartly: "If it is bad for children to be educated exclusively by women, it is also bad for young men and women of college age to be educated exclusively by men. But at the present almost all the colleges prefer as an instructor even a third or fourth rate man to a first rate woman."[51]

Professional teachers' associations continued to ignore their predominantly female membership and restricted women's activity at conferences and meetings. In 1908 the *Woman's Journal* reprinted an article from an education journal that noted that women appeared on the program of a teachers' conference program only if they were musicians or singers.[52] The NEA was as discriminatory as the state associations. Although the *Woman's Journal* applauded the 1895 election of a woman to the post of second vice president of the NEA, the paper noted that this was the first time that the association had selected a woman for such a high post.[53] When the 1903 Annual NEA Conference met in Boston, the *Woman's Journal* commented on the lack of women speakers on the program for the general session; no women appeared on the executive committee; only two were on the advisory committee for the Boston convention; and whereas there were to be 258 addresses by men, women speakers appeared only 34 times.[54] Five years later the *Woman's Journal* reprinted an article from the *Journal of Education* extolling the large number of women speakers at the 1908 conference; but appended to the reprint was the paper's keen observation "that of the twelve newly elected Vice Presidents of NEA, only one is a woman."[55] Undoubtedly much pride and enthusiasm underscored the paper's reporting on the campaign of Ella Flagg Young to become the NEA's first woman president and in 1910 the *Woman's Journal* happily announced that she had been elected 617 to 376 votes.[56]

With the paper's incessant reports on salary differentials between male and female teachers, the lack of career advancement, and the general hostility to women teachers by the public as well as the professional associations, the *Woman's Journal* clearly did not endorse teaching as a good career choice for its readers. Frequently the paper became explicit in its message. In 1870 Lucy Stone described her visit with Mary Mitchell, the first woman graduate of Bates College (Lewiston, Maine). Mitchell had become a high school teacher and told Stone that her salary was $500, whereas her male principal received $3,000 and his male assistant earned $1,800, although she was "their equal in scholarship and ability." Concluding the article, Stone publicly counseled the disgruntled young woman to accept the better paying job offer of proofreader for Greek and Latin textbooks and warned readers: "Women must not drift into the profession of teaching. They must do something that pays better."[57] Not always subtle in its efforts to decrease the oversupply of women in the field, the paper printed articles such as the one applauding the ingenuity of two Buffalo, New York, girls who "instead of adding themselves to the surplus of schoolteachers" opened a dressmaking business which became "successful in a matter of months."[58] In 1908 the paper came down hard on teaching. Titled "Why Women Leave Teaching," the two part series denounced teaching as a poorly paid, expensive profession that no longer attracted the brightest graduates. Not only were the wages inadequate, teaching was also costly. The article reported that a number of school committees required a prospective teacher to submit a list of education periodicals to which she subscribed before being hired; other systems insisted that their teachers attend high-priced summer schools. As an ultimate deterrent, the paper announced that an overworked teacher enjoyed little free time to meet a "husband of good class." Commenting that women teachers often married fellow teachers, often as poor as themselves, the paper declared that nurses and business women has better marital chances because they were in contact with wealthier men.[59]

Material from women's rights papers about women's "true profession" belies the assessment that women teachers were victims of "a nineteenth century 'feminine mystique'," and showed no signs of rebellion against their inferior status within their chosen profession.[60] Using women's rights papers as public forums, women teachers were outraged and outspoken about their treatment in the profession. Far from being quietly resigned to their situation, women teachers used the women's rights periodicals to vent their displeasure and frustration about an expanding number of issues—from pay discrimination to lack of administrative promotions to inability to play meaningful roles in their professional associations.

Women teachers and women's rights periodicals were natural allies. Women teachers were a highly literate group, had a keen personal interest in the attainment of equal rights for women, especially equal pay, and were voiceless in their own profession. In turn, women's rights periodicals needed an audience.

A ready-made group of literate subscribers was women teachers who in 1870 constituted 90 percent of all professional women in America. Many of the editors of the women's rights periodicals had been teachers themselves and were especially sympathetic to the plight of women teachers.

The women's rights periodicals served as nationwide channels of communication for women teachers. Their function was to spread information and increase women's awareness of their subordinate role in the teaching profession. The message proclaimed by the papers was that women teachers were victimized. Unfortunately, the papers seldom advanced plans or solutions to improve women's role. Before a solution can be offered, there must be a general awareness that there is a problem—this was the role of the women's rights press. The periodicals enabled women teachers in schools from New York City to Willamette, Oregon, to voice their concerns, to share experiences, and to know that women were working to improve women's "true profession."

NOTES

1. Horace Mann, "Ninth Annual Report of the Secretary to the Board of Education," *Common School Journal* 8 (April 16, 1846): 118.

2. Sarah Hale, "Woman the Teacher," *Godey's Lady's Book* 37 (September 1848):143–44.

3. Richard Bernard and Maris Vinovskis, "The Female School Teachers in Ante-Bellum Massachusetts," *Journal of Social History* 10 (March 1977):339.

4. *Report of the Commissioner of Education The Year 1880.* (Washington, D.C.: Government Printing Office, 1882), 408–409.

5. Only three editors lacked teaching experience: Paulina Wright Davis of the *Una*, Anne McDowell of the *Woman's Advocate*, and Elizabeth Cady Stanton of the *Revolution*.

6. Samuel Lewis, "Third Annual Report of the Superintendent of Common Schools," *Connecticut Common School Journal* 2 (March 1, 1840):155.

7. *Lily*, April 1, 1855, 52.

8. Willard Elsbree, *The American Teacher: Education of a Profession in a Democracy* (New York: American Book Co., 1939), 254.

9. Edgar Wesley, *NEA: the First Hundred Years: the Building of the Teaching Profession* (New York: Harper & Brothers, 1957), 23. Wesley noted the "chivalrous inconsistency" of the early NEA that permitted

two women to sign the constitution although membership was restricted to "gentlemen." Women could also be elected honorary members and could submit their opinions on issues in the form of written essays, to be read by a male member of the Association.

10. *Lily*, July 1, 1856, 93–94.

11. *Una*, April 1, 1853, 44.

12. *Una*, November 1854, 364.

13. *Una*, May 2, 1853, 63.

14. *Una*, February 1854, 218-219.

15. Janet Hooks, *Women's Occupations Through Seven Decades* (Washington, D.C.: U.S. Department of Labor, 1947; reprint ed., Washington, D.C.: Zenger Publishing Co., 1975), 158.

16. *Revolution*, January 15, 1868, 25–26.

17. *Revolution*, April 23, 1868, 246–247.

18. *Revolution*, April 16, 1868, 227.

19. *Revolution*, April 28, 1870, 268.

20. *Revolution*, July 9, 1869, 3.

21. *Revolution*, February 18, 1869, 101.

22. *Revolution*, December 16, 1869, 380.

23. *Agitator*, April 3, 1869, 8.

24. *Agitator*, June 5, 1869, 5.

25. *Agitator*, June 12, 1869, 5.

26. *Agitator*, July 24, 1869, 8.

27. *Pioneer*, January 5, 1871, 3.

28. Most of the historical research on the issue of married women teachers concentrates on the laws against married women teachers in the 1900s and 1930s, see "Married Women as Teachers," *Educational Review* 25 (February 1903): 213; David Wilbur Peters, *The Status of the Married Woman Teacher* (New York: Teachers College, 1934); and Patricia Carter, "A Coalition Between Women Teachers and the Feminist Movement in New York City, 1900–1920," Ed.D. diss., University of Cincinnati, 1985. However, in reading articles from the women's rights press, it is obvious that restrictions on married women teachers were in effect at least thirty years before their adoption in New York City.

29. *Pioneer*, May 28, 1870, 3.

30. *New Northwest*, November 10, 1876, 2.

31. *New Northwest*, August 23, 1883, 6.

32. *Queen Bee*, February 19, 1890. Sexual harassment, a problem experienced frequently by young women teachers, remains undocumented. For a rare first-hand account of the problem among Vermont school teachers in the early twentieth century, see Margaret Nelson, "The Threat of Sexual Harassment: Rural Vermont School Teachers,

1915–1950" (Paper delivered at the Annual Meeting of the American Educational Research Association, New Orleans, April 1984).

33. *Woman's Chronicle*, July 25, 1891, 1.
34. *Woman's Tribune*, September 1, 1888, 1.
35. *Woman's Journal*, January 8, 1870, 3.
36. *Woman's Journal*, February 5, 1870, 34.
37. *Woman's Journal*, April 22, 1911, 122.
38. *Woman's Journal*, August 5, 1916, 256.
39. *Woman's Journal*, January 6, 1916, 6.
40. *Woman Citizen*, March 6, 1920, 964.
41. *Woman's Journal*, October 15, 1870, 322.
42. *Woman's Journal*, September 19, 1874, 306.
43. *Woman's Journal*, September 8, 1883, 281.
44. For a description of the "woman peril" in the schools, see Thomas Woody, *A History of Women's Education in the United States*, 2 vols. (New York: Science Press, 1929), 1:505–514.
45. *Woman's Journal*, May 4, 1872, 144.
46. *Woman's Journal*, March 12, 1892, 86.
47. *Woman's Journal*, April 2, 1892, 108.
48. *Woman's Journal*, April 19, 1902, 126–127.
49. *Woman's Journal*, April 19, 1902, 124.
50. The findings of the Mosely Commission consist of twenty-seven individual reports and take up over 400 pages. A summary of the report written by W. T. Harris appeared in the *Report of the Commissioner of Education for the Year Ending 1905*, 2 vols. (Washington, D.C.: Government Printing Office, 1909),1:1–39.
51. *Woman's Journal*, May 7, 1904, 148.
52. *Woman's Journal*, March 29, 1908, 52.
53. *Woman's Journal*, August 24, 1895, 268.
54. *Woman's Journal*, June 13, 1903, 185.
55. *Woman's Journal*, July 25, 1908, 120.
56. *Woman's Journal*, July 9, 1910, 10.
57. *Woman's Journal*, August 20, 1870, 260.
58. *Woman's Journal*, June 12, 1886, 185.
59. *Woman's Journal*, August 1, 1908, 122; August 29, 1908, 140.
60. Keith Melder, "Woman's High Calling: the Teaching Profession in America, 1830–1860," *American Studies* 13 (Fall 1972):19–32.

5

PROFESSIONAL AND GRADUATE EDUCATION OF WOMEN

Although teaching swiftly became women's "true profession," the domains of medicine, law, dentistry, college teaching, and graduate education were considerably less accessible to female aspirants. Influential ladies' magazines touted teaching as an eminently suitable occupation for women but firmly cautioned readers against vying with men for professional positions. Articles counseled the female reader to shun the worldly vocations of men because "her natural delicacy will shrink from the rude contact of such boisterous occupations."[1]

The authors of the 1848 Declaration of Sentiments publicly challenged those genteel proscriptions when they wrote: "He has monopolized nearly all the profitable employments, and from those she is permitted to follow, she receives but a scanty remuneration. He closes against her all the avenues to wealth and distinction which he considers most honorable to himself. As a teacher of theology, medicine, or law, she is not known."[2] Women's rights activists disputed those who said women's minds were too weak for serious intellectual pursuits, their bodies too delicate for strenuous endeavors, and their emotions too refined to deal with the harsh world outside the home. They encouraged women to aspire to positions offering money, power, and a public role because as Julia Ward Howe, the well-known reformer, succinctly remarked: "The professions indeed supply the key-stone to the arch of woman's liberty."[3]

Women professionals were universally scorned. It was not uncommon for family, friends, and society to stigmatize them as biological defectives or social misfits. Women's rights papers were the only group to publicly commend their ambitions. Aware that the role of all women would be enhanced if a significant number of women gained power and status through admission to highly regarded, well-paying positions, women's rights papers campaigned vigorously for their inclusion.

The beginnings of women professionals and women's rights papers were intertwined by both time and geography. Twenty-two days after the inaugural copies of the *Lily* rolled off the press in Seneca Falls, New York, in nearby Geneva, Elizabeth Blackwell received the first M.D. degree ever conferred on a woman by an American medical school.[4] Blackwell's medical degree formally marked women's entrance into the learned professions; but progress was to be slow and laborious. In an 1869 editorial in a medical journal a male doctor wrote: "If I were to plan with malicious hate the greatest curse I could conceive for woman, if I would estrange them from the protection of woman, and make them as far as possible loathsome and disgusting to man, I would favor the so-called reform which proposed to make doctors of them."[5] That piece displayed the depth of emotion about women doctors and could be applied to all women professionals. Despite the writer's desire, women doctors were not to be "estranged" from the protection of all women. Women's rights papers enveloped them with a support system offering abundant advice, comfort, and most of all encouragement.

Ironically, in the *Lily's* first article advocating women doctors, editor Bloomer argued not on the principle of equal rights but on the grounds of female "delicacy." This line of thinking contended that examinations by male doctors outraged women's innate modesty and was repeatedly employed by women's rights supporters as well as those unsympathetic to the movement. Bloomer made no mention of women's natural right to become doctors, but instead drew on deeply held emotions:

There is always something abhorrent in the thought of having to send for a *man*, if you are a little indisposed, and may be subjected to his inquisitiveness. Many a lady we believe, had rather suffer much—and in many instances, does, to her great injury—rather than undergo the necessary investigation of disease from physicians. But give her one of her own sex, and how much more easily could she unburden her sorrows, and how much more readily would they be understood.[6]

Whether out of respect for female modesty or regard for equal rights, in 1850 the Female Medical College of Pennsylvania (renamed the Woman's Medical College of Pennsylvania in 1867) was founded as the first medical college for women. In announcing that fifty women comprised the college's first class, the *Lily* optimistically proclaimed "Clear the way, ye gentlemen doctors, the women are coming."[7]

Early women's rights supporters focused on the numerical production of women doctors rather than on the environment in which they were trained. In 1851 the *Lily* reported that Harvard's medical department admitted three "colored men" and one woman. However, because of violent student protests over the woman's admission, she withdrew.[8] Although the paper usually disparaged all-female institutions, the article concluded with the comment, "We think female medical students should patronize their own colleges."[9]

Davis, editor of the *Una*, disagreed with that sentiment. In an article describing her visit to the Female Medical College of Pennsylvania, Davis contended that mediocre training, inadequate facilities and equipment, and lower standards were endemic to schools for women. She favored coeducational medical schools because she feared that ill-prepared women doctors would doom the progress of women in the profession. Addressing male readers, Davis queried: "Shall women who are to have charge of your wives, your children, and your sisters be inadequately filled for their work? Will you entrust your loved ones to those who have less opportunities for education, than you demand in the man who is to take charge of your life when disease visits you?"[10]

In the paper's next issue, Dr. Ellwood Harvey, a professor at the Philadelphia institution, took issue with Davis's description of deficiencies. In the school's defense, Harvey claimed that the college gave thirty more lectures per session than did the all-male medical department at the University of Pennsylvania and that extensive collections of museum models and anatomical specimens were available to the female students.[11] Following Harvey's assertion of high standards, the unappeased Davis appended an editorial calling for coeducational medical schools and concluded: "Were colleges at once endowed for women, richer and higher in every respect than those for men, we would only protest the more earnestly against them, for we only ask for equality in all respects."[12]

Because irregular or eclectic medical schools readily admitted women students, women's rights papers did not embroil themselves in the intense rivalry between regular and irregular schools of medicine.[13] Women's rights paper's overriding objective was that medical schools admit and treat women fairly and on this point it was the irregular or eclectic schools who met that standard. Before 1861 the majority of women who received medical training or degrees attended eclectic or other irregular institutions because the regular medical schools refused to accept them as students.[14] The eclectic schools were extraordinarily influential in the production of women doctors as shown by a *Woman's Advocate* article on the New York Hydropathic and Physiological School (New York City). At its 1856 commencement ceremony, the irregular medical school graduated thirty males and twenty females. All students received the same instruction and were taught by male and female faculty members.[15]

Although female physicians numbered less than 200 among the 55,055 male physicians in 1860, the medical profession had already instituted a many-sided campaign to discourage women doctors.[16] Not content to refuse women admittance to medical colleges, the profession attempted to bar students in the female medical colleges from clinical experience. Male doctors argued that exposing women to the blood and agony of wards and operating rooms was "indecent." In 1856 the *Woman's Advocate* reported that students from the Female Medical College of Pennsylvania were no longer permitted to observe surgical operations at Pennsylvania Hospital. Deeming the restriction "miserable and narrow minded," editor McDowell informed readers that such a practice denied women medical students vital professional knowledge.[17]

The Civil War eased some of the opposition to women's involvement in the public sphere. When men enlisted in the two armies, women assumed a number of occupations outside the home, from nursing to office work to government service. They found these occupations exhilarating and gained a sense of accomplishment and self worth.[18] At the war's end, women's newly won confidence persisted, their sphere widened, and they began to make inroads into professions other than medicine.

With the surge in the number of coeducational institutions, the *Revolution* proudly announced a woman had become a member of the faculty at coeducational Albion College (Albion, Michigan).[19] While academia and medicine grudgingly admitted women, law resolutely resisted their advances.[20] Women lawyers did not appear until the late 1860s and then in very small numbers. In 1869 Arabella Mansfield passed the Iowa State Bar and officially became recognized as the first woman lawyer in the United States. It is estimated that in 1870 no more than four women were attending U.S. law schools. Although the number of law schools admitting women increased, by 1890 the figures for women in the law had not altered dramatically and the estimated figure, combining all women lawyers and all women law students, was placed at 135.[21]

Women dentists were another rare professional group.[22] To encourage more women into the field, the *Revolution* printed an autobiographical account written by an unnamed German woman who attended the Pennsylvania College of Dental Surgery (Philadelphia). Although a heated debate preceded her admission, the writer reported that students and faculty quickly became friendly. It was difficult to be the only female in the school, and "only the thought that my success would incite other women to do likewise, and that I might be of some use to my German sisters, strengthened me, and enabled me to surmount every difficulty." After completing the course, she established a thriving practice. Appended to her account was a letter from James Truman, one of her professors, who aroused antagonism among his colleagues by publicly championing the fitness of women to practice dentistry. Truman wrote that as a student the woman worked diligently, following the same six to eight hour day of lectures and labs taken by her male peers. After praising her outstanding adeptness at performing operations, he concluded: "One single proof like this of the capacity of woman for a more liberal education refutes a thousand theoretical objections of narrow scholars."[23]

Despite testimonials to their ability, women were generally not welcomed in any of the professions. In 1868 the *Revolution* printed a speech delivered by Henry James to the Woman's Club of Boston. Opposed to women in the professions, especially those in the clergy and law, James declared: "It is degrading to a woman to preach or argue because these functions are essentially combative; and it is her prerogative to conquer without combat." In an atypical editorial comment at the conclusion of James's inflammatory statement, Elizabeth Cady Stanton serenely wrote: "Please remember that with woman all things are possible . . . When woman enters the professions, she will do for them what she has already done for the literature of the age in which we live; for the true woman must elevate and ennoble whatever she touches, and beautify every path in which she walks."[24]

With her usual verve, Stanton welcomed the first copy of the *Agitator* with the rousing call: "We must stir up the girls everywhere to crowd into the colleges and professions, profitable trades and political offices, and thus decrease the supply of laborers for schools and sewing machines, and thereby raise the wages of all."[25] Heeding Stanton's message, the *Agitator* filled its pages with career information, primarily on women and the medical profession. Letters from successful women graduates of medical schools contained both information and inspiration. Sarah Chase of Berea, Ohio, informed readers that she was enrolled at coeducational Western Homeopathic College (Cleveland). Both students and faculty treated women with respect and Chase invited women to write her if they had any questions about medicine as a career.[26] Chase received so many inquiries that she had to respond via the paper than with individual letters. Her column addressed the wide-ranging questions. To prepare for medical school, she suggested that women study chemistry and English and she recommended purchase of a "set of bones and *Gray's Anatomy*." After detailing the curriculum of her college, she added that although the institution was not well-equipped, it was eager to enroll women students.[27]

All women's rights papers contained numerous references to the generous salaries earned by women doctors, an indication that money was a compelling factor in women's decisions to chose medicine. In an unsigned letter to the *Agitator*, a pioneer "super woman," wrote that she had recently graduated from the Hygeio-Therapeutic College (Florence, New Jersey). She established her practice in the West and after only three months claimed earnings of $330. Obviously meant to inspire others, she noted that during her first week of her new practice she cared for her family of five, bought a house, purchased all her household goods, made a carpet, tended patients and earned $36.50![28]

The *Agitator* briefly noted women's advances in other professions. Law news was mixed. An account of the admission of Arabella Mansfield to the Iowa Bar in 1869 was followed by information that the law department of Columbia (New York City) refused to admit two women students.[29] The paper reported a major breakthrough for women dentists when it announced that at its 1869 annual meeting the American Dental Association officially admitted women to the profession.[30] Women college faculty also met with some success. Beginning its article with the lead "Honor to that University," the *Agitator* reported that a twenty-one-year-old college graduate, Martha Baldwin, had been appointed professor of Greek and Latin at the University of Kansas (Lawrence, Kansas).[31]

Only a few reprints from eastern papers on women in the professions appeared in the *Pioneer*, indicating that the topic of professional women was not one of the paper's prime concerns. Another western paper, the *New Northwest* took more interest in women's professional advances. When a much publicized article in a British medical journal claimed that women would never confide in a female physician, editor Duniway disputed the contention. Employing terminology used by the *Lily* thirty years before, Duniway stated that women often felt degraded by having to reveal "delicate" information to a male physician. Reverting back to her more forthright manner, she concluded her discussion by candidly addressing an unspoken but underlying issue behind much criticism of women doctors. Duniway stated: "We feel that physicians, as well as politicians, are quaking in their boots over the prospect of dividing emoluments with women; else they would not resort to scandal and subterfuge in their endeavors to keep back or intimidate the fast increasing numbers of women physicians."[32]

Even medical schools that accepted women engaged in the "intimidation" to which Duniway referred. An Oregon reader wrote describing the opening ceremony at the Medical University of Willamette (Oregon), which enrolled two women students. After commenting on all of the speeches praising the many noble men of the medical profession and the prayers imploring divine help for the men aspiring to become doctors, the correspondent, most likely one of the two women students, bitterly remarked: "The whole procedure virtually said 'We admit you to the college because we are compelled to do so, but in heart we ignore you'."[33] A second letter detailed additional "intimidations, including the practice in which professors always referred to fretful or disagreeable patients as "she or her." [34]

Even the militant *Queen Bee* evidenced some traditional thinking about women in medicine. When a woman doctor, A. B. Stockman, wrote to urge more women into medicine, she offered conventional advice to those contemplating the unconventional career. Aware that women doctors were criticized for straying too far from acceptable norms of female conduct, Stockman emphasized that a woman doctor "must be a lady, a womanly woman. No aping of masculine habits, dress or foibles will conduce to success."[35] Editor Churchill, a resolute women's rights supporter, herself proffered traditional thoughts on why women should become doctors. Following an 1883 article announcing the opening of the next session of the Woman's Medical College of St. Louis, Missouri, Churchill declared that women: "are peculiarly fitted by nature and their social position to relieve the sufferings of those of their own sex, and of children."[36] Nine years later Churchill's thinking had progressed beyond ideas of women's innate healing instincts. In an 1892 article praising women dentists, Churchill stated: "It is not because woman is better adapted to the work of dentistry than to other departments of activity that she is so successful. In what ever direction she turns her hand she meets with success. When woman ceases to be dependent, she will achieve glory."[37]

Although the number of women doctors soared from 544 in 1870 to 4,557 in 1890, the *Woman's Journal* never stopped promoting the concept that medicine was a suitable profession for them.[38] Famous women authored columns of inspiration and encouragement. In 1870 Caroline Dall, the former corresponding editor of the *Una* and an active crusader on women's issues, produced an extensive essay heralding women's contributions to medicine, tracing them back to antiquity. She concluded: "When we consider the persistent opposition of men and the want of general education (among women), have we any reason to be ashamed of the record?"[39]

Ten years later Emily Blackwell, a doctor like her sister Elizabeth Blackwell, authored a similar piece. However, women had advanced so much that she was able to cite names of contemporary American women doctors rather than relying on examples from Ancient Rome and Egypt. Blackwell described how she and her sister had founded the Woman's Medical College of the New York Infirmary for Women and Children (New York City), which during its twelve-year history produced forty-six women doctors. Blackwell commented that most of the women graduates practiced, earned good incomes, and "accumulated an independence." Concluding her article she announced that medicine was "one of the most remunerative careers for women."[40]

Like other women's rights papers, the *Woman's Journal* kept a keen eye on the monetary rewards of the medical profession and was not reticent about promoting that message. In 1881 the paper reprinted Dean Rachel Bodley's commencement address to the twenty-nine new graduates of the Woman's Medical College of Pennsylvania. Rather than simply reaffirming women's claims to practice medicine, Bodley delineated tangible accomplishments of alumnae of her institution. Over three decades, the school produced 276 women doctors and 189 of them responded to a survey concerning their professional lives. Bodley summarized the major findings: 109 of the 189 respondents reported that they were in practice, usually in northern cities and most often worked in obstetrics or gynecology or in a combination of those two specialties with a general practice. Bodley reported that their average salary was $2,907, three times that of a male white collar worker of the era, and that four of the women earned between $15,000 and $20,000 a year. Never one to let such good news pass without comment, the *Woman's Journal* boasted: "Almost $3000 a year income for the average woman, when equipped with a knowledge of medicine! Without this despised 'higher education' the average woman would wash dishes and patch, at an income of about $150, or dawdle through the year at no income, and the expenditure of all that paternal or other charity would bestow upon her. The country has a profit in the full education of its girls."[41]

Reports such as Bodley's may have inspired many women to consider medicine as a profession, but it undoubtedly fanned great opposition to women doctors by males in the profession. Whether provoked by women's disregard for their traditional domestic role or by monetary concerns, the medical profession erected formidable barriers against women doctors. These discriminatory practices, and their subversions by women, were well documented in the *Woman's Journal*.

The all-male medical school of Harvard was an important bastion for women's rights activists to storm. Harvard was for men only. Aware that the Boston institution was a bellwether for other medical colleges to adopt coeducation, in 1878 Mary Hovey, a Boston heiress, offered Harvard $10,000 if it would open its doors to women medical students. The Hovey grant was an example of "creative or coercive philanthropy," a powerful lever that women would use again to open institutions to women.[42] In May 1879, after a year-long debate, Harvard Medical College faculty voted thirteen to five against admitting women—aversion to women doctors triumphed over avarice. The Hovey grant and the ensuing debate over its acceptance was covered in the *Woman's Journal*, and by July 1879 the paper resigned itself to the fact that admittance of women to the Harvard Medical School was a dead issue.[43]

Even when women cleared the hurdles of acceptance to and graduation from medical college, they faced additional discrimination. Admittance to a medical society was the next barrier. Admission to a medical society confirmed a physician's abilities, secured cooperation and referrals from other doctors, and was often a prerequisite for admission to the staffs of hospitals. Being a member of a medical society was vital to the career of women doctors, and it was a frequent topic in the

Woman's Journal. Denials of membership to women doctors were publicized and condemned. Under the strident headline "War on the Woman Physicians," an 1870 article reported that the State Medical Society of Pennsylvania refused to recognize graduates of female medical colleges as members.[44] Throughout the 1870s the *Woman's Journal* noted denials of memberships by other city and state medical societies, including Massachusetts, which did not admit women until 1884.[45]

As women teachers played second-class roles at their professional conferences, a similar fate befell women doctors. In 1881 Mary Livermore reported on the Seventh International Medical Conference held in London. Attended by over 2,400 physicians from all over the world, the conference barred women doctors from all meetings, including sessions on obstetrics and diseases of women and children, the usual domains of women doctors. Livermore concluded wearily: "It is the same story everywhere. Every step of woman's advancement is opposed and yielded only after a struggle. Man, who styles himself 'woman's Natural Protector' makes the way hard for her, and hinders where he should help."[46]

Despite the barrage of opposition to women physicians, their numbers were far greater than for any of the other traditionally male professions. In 1870 there were more women doctors in Boston than there were women lawyers in the entire nation.[47] Although 1869 saw the first woman admitted to practice before a state bar, that event did not signal a massive influx of women into the legal profession. Throughout the 1870s and 1880s women were refused admission to the bar in a number of states, and only a few law schools admitted women.

The traditional argument, cited whenever women attempted to enter a profession, contended that women's professional role would interfere with her primary duty as wife and mother. With few role models to emulate and intense resistance against them, it is not surprising that only a small number of women chose to become lawyers in the nineteenth century. Although articles on women in the law were fewer than those on women in medicine, the *Woman's Journal* did much to counsel women contemplating the legal profession. In 1875 Lavinia Goodell, who had been refused admission to the Wisconsin Bar on the grounds of sex, authored an article for the *Woman's Journal*. Intended to provide guidance for aspiring young women lawyers, Goodell suggested that if a young woman had only the faintest interest in the law, she should immediately begin to adopt a simpler style of dress, to forsake popular novels and magazines, and begin to read law. In her opinion, college courses were "helpful but not indispensable" and one could easily obtain legal education outside law school. In contrast to the frequent reports of comfortable salaries received by women doctors, Goodell stated that the practice of law was not immediately remunerative and that it took a number of years to build a good practice.[48]

A woman dentist from Philadelphia produced a similar piece for women considering her specialization. After analyzing the merits of a number of coeducational dental schools, the author promised women "profit and enjoyment" in the profession. To substantiate her claim, she cited the example of Henrietta Hirschfeld, a graduate of Pennsylvania College of Dental Surgery, who returned to her native Germany and had the Prussian crown princess as one of her patients.[49]

Female role models in all of the professions were essential and college and university classrooms were targeted as incubators of role models in the professions. A *Woman's Journal* correspondent sagely noted: "There must be women professors where there are women students before these institutions can furnish for our girls the best and highest education."[50] Few coeducational colleges employed women as faculty members and if they did women were found at the lower ranks. A Kansas reader commented on the lack of women full professors at the University of Kansas (Lawrence). Describing a situation similar to that endured by women teachers in public schools, the angry reader declared that the University of Kansas paid its women faculty $1,200 a year, whereas male professors received between $1,800 to $3,000. In response to questions concerning this pay differential, she reported that one member of the governing board remarked: "The place of women is naturally subordinate."[51]

Moving women into professorial ranks became a goal of the women's rights press and they pressured graduate schools to produce women doctorates. Although Yale established graduate courses in philosophy and the arts as early as 1846 and awarded the nation's first Ph.D. degrees in 1861, and Harvard founded its Graduate School of Arts and Sciences in 1872, graduate schools did not become significant institutions on American campuses until the 1890s. During their formative years, graduate schools followed the pattern of undergraduate institutions, and reluctantly admitted women. Although spurned at home, many women followed the example of men and pursued graduate study abroad, most often in Germany, Switzerland, and France.

In 1885 Florence Kelley Wischnewetzky wrote a two-part article for the *Woman's Journal* describing her experiences as an American woman graduate student at the University of Zurich. Although all schools of the university admitted women, the majority of American women were found in the schools of medicine and philosophy. A few were in the law school and none in the school of theology. Wischnewetzky suggested that women interested in studying at the Swiss university should be familiar with authors such as Smith, Ricardo, and Mill.[52] Her second letter detailed the specifics of Zurich's medical school, which was attended by a number of women graduates of American medical schools seeking the clinical and hospital experience often denied them in America. Despite their possession of American medical degrees, Wischnewetzky declared that most of her countrywomen lacked basic scientific training and consequently learned little from the courses. She concluded her letter with a call to abolish women's medical colleges in America because she believed that coeducational medical education provided women with a superior background.[53] Wischnewetzky's comments showed that remnants of the debate of coeducational versus all-female medical schools existed. She may have been correct in her assessment of the inferior training in female medical colleges of the period, and in fact many had already closed or merged with coeducational medical schools in the 1870s. However, such institutions were vital to the preparation of women doctors because many schools continued to refuse to admit women or admitted them in small numbers. As late as 1892, 63 percent of all women enrolled in regular medical colleges were attending the remaining seven female ones.[54]

The attainment of graduate degrees, both abroad or in America, involved considerable expense, and beginning in the 1850s promising male college graduates were encouraged to begin graduate study by receiving fellowships. These fellowships gave them funds to take courses and attain advanced degrees needed to teach in colleges and universities. Women saw fellowships as a means to increase the number of women college faculty. In 1884, thirty years after men received such awards, Cornell University awarded the first fellowship to a woman, Harriet Grotecloss.[55] The *Woman's Journal* recognized the importance of fellowships for women. In 1888 the paper published a letter from Cora Benneson, a graduate of the University of Michigan and a Fellow in History at Bryn Mawr College's new graduate program. Benneson announced that fellowships intended to fund advanced study and promote the development of women college professors were available. Inexplicably, she did not mention who funded them or how one attained them. She noted that there were eight women fellows at Cornell, six at Bryn Mawr, and one at Wesleyan.[56] Funding graduate women gained support and several months after Benneson's letter, the *Woman's Journal* reported that the Association of Collegiate Alumnae (later known as the American Association of University Women) planned to award fellowships to women for advanced study in both America and Europe.[57]

In 1890 women composed 35 percent of the undergraduate population. After receiving B.A. degrees, these educated young women faced a dilemma concerning their after-college life. They aspired to more stimulating occupations than that of reclining in fern-filled parlors discussing the latest fashions or laboring over a needlework project. However, the societal role of an educated woman was in flux and a deep disjunction between college life and cultural expectations existed. *After College, What,* a popular advice manual published in 1896, urged new alumnae to overcome the "blank nothingness" that often followed four stimulating collegiate years by adopting some useful activity, "something to do."[58] Women's rights papers were more explicit in their advice and encouraged women graduates to venture into the professions or to attend graduate school.

In 1891 the *Woman's Chronicle* reported on a plan to admit women to the Johns Hopkins Medical School (Baltimore, Maryland). The scheme resembled the "coercive philanthropy" used in 1878 during an attempt to coeducate Harvard Medical School; however in the case of Johns Hopkins it succeeded.[59] Mary Garrett, heiress to the Baltimore and Ohio Railroad fortune, offered Johns Hopkins University a gift of $60,000 if the institution admitted women to its soon to be opened medical school. Noting that opposition to the gift was intense, the *Woman's Chronicle* argued in its usual conservative voice that since "nursing has long been conceded as belonging in a great measure to woman's sphere, then why not permit her to become fully equipped for the perfect work of healing?"[60] Garrett's offer was not immediately accepted, and two years later the paper reported that Garrett increased the gift to $306,000. The trustees, anxious to open the school, agreed to her conditions and appointed a committee of six women to oversee questions affecting the female medical students.[61]

The report on the Garrett gift was an anomaly for the southern paper. Articles in the *Woman's Chronicle* on women's forays into the professions were infrequent and largely of regional interest. The *Woman's Tribune* displayed a more national perspective. Sex discrimination at medical schools was highly publicized. An anonymous friend described the difficulties of Mary Wolfe, a female medical student at Pulte Medical College (Cincinnati, Ohio), to the *Woman's Tribune*. Following a series of incidents intended to force Wolfe to leave the school, including the burning of one of her examination papers by a professor, Wolfe's father filed law suits against the medical school and the professor. He won, Wolfe was allowed to graduate, and her friend triumphantly reported that Wolfe was now well established as an assistant in her father's practice.[62] Another account was more pessimistic. In 1892 Lena Whitcomb, a student at Hahnemann Medical College (Chicago), complained that no woman medical student had ever been selected to be either house surgeon or physician.[63] Her complaint was a valid one. Although not an important element of early nineteenth-century medical education, by the late 1890s and early 1900s, an internship became almost mandatory before a doctor could establish a practice. In a "catch 22" situation, women's inability to secure internships was often used as a reason for refusal to admit them to medical schools.[64]

The paper encouraged comments from readers because they provided personal insights into problems and issues. At the conclusion of her letter on how to be a proper foreign graduate student, Agnes Kemp, a student at the University of Zurich, noted that most of the women graduate students were either American or Russian. Complaining that European women were too engrossed in caring for men or producing elaborate needlework to undertake graduate studies, she declared: "They seem as yet unawakened to the higher possibilities of intellectual, social, political, and spiritual life."[65]

In her criticism of the lack of intellectual ambition among European women, Kemp overlooked the power of male disapproval to deter women's educational advances. An example of this was reported in 1893 by Ada Frederikson, an American student at the Sorbonne. Frederikson told *Woman's Tribune* readers that she and other women students were constantly subjected to obscene songs and charges that they should leave the French university and go home to cook dinner. Insults were leveled by students as well as faculty, and she reported that when one professor encountered a woman attending his class he began a lecture on the theme that educated women never find husbands.[66]

Overlooking the societal backlash against educated women, the *Woman's Journal* of the 1890s exuded optimism and confidence that women professionals were established and no longer scorned or challenged. An example of upbeat message appeared in 1890 when the *Woman's Journal* responded to an article from the *New England Monthly* in which a male doctor claimed that few women doctors maintained practices because they lacked stamina. At the reprint's conclusion there was no refutation of his charges; instead the paper jauntily dismissed his attack by writing: "Why load our guns to shoot a mosquito?" The *Woman's Journal* boasted that the increasing number of coeducational medical schools and female medical students, as well as the increase in the number of women's names in the medical directories of large cities was more than sufficient evidence to dispel his charges.[67]

The paper's satisfaction about the progress of women doctors was most apparent in its fiction columns. During this era, the *Woman's Journal* printed several stories dealing with talented women doctors, each showing a progressive growth of career confidence. In 1894 "How Anne Convinced Her Father" told the story of doctor's daughter who became a doctor despite his objections. At the story's end she married a fellow doctor who "did not deem Anne any the less worthy because of her professional skill."[68] In 1904 "Dr. Mary's Engagement" related the saga of a beautiful young woman doctor who requested a year's engagement from her wealthy lawyer fiance while she established herself as the main physician in an almshouse. When Dr. Mary discovered that an ill, impoverished patient was her fiance's mother, she canceled the planned marriage, declaring nobly that his heartless treatment of his mother showed he "can be no fit husband to any woman."[69] In 1919 a story captured the essence of the "new woman" when it related the adventures of a successful woman doctor who was also a brilliant speaker, an enthusiastic suffragist, a civic worker, and, of course, "a beauty." When this multitalented paragon was asked to forsake her career for marriage, she responded in true "new woman" style. She agreed to the marriage but refused to give up her career, stating: "You can't shelve a career as if it didn't count for two whoops."[70]

By the 1900s it was evident that the *Woman's Journal* believed that all the problems of women in medicine had been solved. Articles highlighting discrimination disappeared and slight, often quite belated, honors were presented as great victories. In 1901 the *Woman's Journal* announced that two women were appointed to head two sections of the North Carolina Medical Society and magnanimously commented: "As the number of women practicing medicine in North Carolina is not large, this is a generous division of the work."[71]

In 1920 the *Woman Citizen* printed a summation of the accomplishments of women doctors given by Sarah McNutt to a banquet of the New York Women's State Medical Society. McNutt, like the paper, took an optimistic view of women's status in medicine. She stated that there were now over forty coeducational medical colleges and women were being named interns at large hospitals. Women doctors were on the staffs of major hospitals and were faculty at prominent medical schools such as Cornell and Harvard. She also noted that one-third of the 6,000 registered female physicians in the country registered during World War I for war relief work and many were decorated for outstanding service by foreign governments.[72]

Similarly, the paper's reports on women in the law were upbeat. In 1891 the *Woman's Journal* announced that twelve women were attending the law school for women attached to the University of the City of New York.[73] Prominent in the paper were reports of successful women lawyers such as Sarah Andrew, a former teacher and a graduate of the Law School of Washington University (St. Louis, Missouri), who was now in joint partnership with her son and Annette Abbott Adams who had been appointed state district attorney in California.[74]

Reports on women in academia were not as auspicious. In 1891 Isabelle Oakley provided unhappy statistics. Oberlin College employed few women faculty and none held the title of full professor. There were only twenty-six women faculty members at the University of Wisconsin and none of the women held rank above that of assistant professor.[75] In 1900 the *Woman's Journal* reported that the trustees of Cornell declared that no woman could become a member of the faculty. This act provoked Louise Brownell, warden of the female dormitory, to resign in protest. Commenting on the Cornell incident, the *Woman's Journal* asserted that such a rule was a "discouragement to the young women students, an object in contempt for women to the young men, and a piece of the same stupid injustice that bars out all women from the ballot box."[76]

Beginning in 1916 the tone of reporting on women college faculty took on the optimism found in articles on women in medicine and law. The paper was filled with the names of newly appointed "first" women faculty at prestigious colleges: in 1916 Yale named Dr. Rhoda Erdman, a lecturer in biology at the graduate school, as its first woman faculty member and Johns Hopkins University appointed Florence Bamberger an instructor of education, its first woman faculty member outside of the institution's medical school.[77] In 1919 the *Woman Citizen* announced that Harvard's first woman faculty member was Dr Alice Hamilton, who was named assistant professor of industrial medicine in the Medical School.[78] The paper was pleased that Harvard had finally capitulated to women's demands for faculty appointments; however, it neglected to report or did not know the unequal conditions of Hamilton's employment. Hamilton was an outstanding "first" woman at Harvard, but even she felt the force of discrimination and her experiences undoubtedly typified those of many of the other "first" women. In order not to disturb Harvard's traditions, Hamilton, as a condition of her employment, agreed not to join the Harvard Club, use special faculty seating at football games, or sit on the platform at commencement. She also never rose above the rank of assistant professor during her sixteen years at the medical school.[79]

From the 1890s onward, women's rights papers focused their efforts on securing the ballot rather than promoting women's professional progress. Although the *Woman's Journal* continued to report news on women in the professions, its tone changed. Optimism and satisfaction dominated. There were few reports of setbacks and no traces of contempt or scorn. Fierce rebuttals to articles disparaging to women professionals and rebukes of professional associations for ignoring women diminished. The paper simply recorded all of women's accomplishments and downplayed any professional discrimination.

With the advent of the twentieth century, women's rights papers, most notably the *Woman's Journal*, viewed women's places in the professions and graduate education with pride and a sense that they were poised on the brink of equality. In many ways they were correct. Statistics from 1900 to 1920 support their optimistic assumptions. By 1920 women were 5 percent of the medical profession, 3.4 percent of all dentists, 1.4 percent of the legal profession; they were 30 percent of college and university faculty, and one in seven doctorates was received by a woman.[80] However, deeper scrutiny of the figures reveals that although women had made considerable progress, their proportion compared to the total figures of those in the professions and graduate schools remained quite small. A close look showed that there was a long way to go before true equality could be claimed.

Between 1890 and 1920 many women chose to regard the increase in the number of professional women and graduate degrees earned by women as signs of great accomplishment. Such an attitude was reflected in the pages of the *Woman's Journal*, the only women's rights paper published after 1909. The paper reduced its coverage of women in the professions and in graduate school and printed only good news on their progress. The paper was no longer an open forum for women to discuss professional discrimination and public scorn. Instead it simply recorded women's accomplishments and never asked if things could be improved.[81]

The paper's attitude reflected the sentiments of the women's movement as a whole. In 1901 Carrie Chapman Catt, the new president of the National American Woman Suffrage Association, wrote a piece for the *Woman's Journal*. Catt hailed the increase in the number of professional women over the past sixty years. Applauding women for taking "a useful and permanent place in all intellectual pursuits and avocations," Catt prophesied: "The twentieth century is destined to see forever eliminated the barbarous restriction of sex in industry."[82]

It is easy to understand why both the *Woman's Journal* and the women's movement were so encouraged by women's progress in the profession. In 1849 Elizabeth Blackwell was the only professional woman in America, yet seventy-one years later women were evident in virtually every field. Society had become more accepting of women, and women's aspirations had broadened. A factor in the metamorphosis of "true women" into professional women and graduate students was the women's rights press. The papers urged women to enter professions, to study abroad, and to compete for graduate school fellowships. They provided women with vital information and inspiring role models, defended them against attacks, and lavished them with moral support. Women professionals, whom society regarded as traitors to their sex, were supported and praised by the women's rights press. Professional women and the women's rights papers worked diligently to enlarge women's sphere and succeeded to some degree. However, their joint dream of one sphere for the sexes was not to be realized, and professional equality, just as social equality, remained elusive.

NOTES

1. William B. Taylor, "Female Influence," *Ladies' Garland* 3 (1840): 188.
2. Susan B. Anthony, Elizabeth Cady Stanton, and Matilda J. Gage, *History of Woman Suffrage*, 6 vols. (New York: Fowler & Wells, 1881–1922), 1:71.

3. Julia Ward Howe, "Introduction," in Annie Nathan Meyer, *Woman's Work in America* (New York: Henry Holt, 1891), 2.

4. For Blackwell's account of her two years of study at Geneva Medical College (now Hobart College), see Elizabeth Blackwell, *Pioneer Work in Opening the Medical Profession to Women: Autobiographical Sketches* (London: Longmans, Green, 1895; reprint ed., New York: Schocken Books, 1977), 64–92.

5. Quoted in Meyer, *Woman's Work in America*, 143.

6. *Lily*, December 1849, 94.

7. *Lily*, October 1850, 45. For a history of this landmark women's medical college, see Guilielma Fell Alsop, *History of the Woman's Medical College, Philadelphia, Pennsylvania, 1850–1950* (Philadelphia: Lippincott, 1950).

8. Although the article did not mention the name of the woman involved in the Harvard incident, it related the facts of the dismissal of Harriot Hunt from Harvard Medical College. Hunt, who applied to the school at age forty-five, was viewed by the faculty as a dignified matron who would not enflame the sexual passions of male students. However, her acceptance enraged the male students, already irate over the admission of three blacks, who called for Hunt's dismissal. Before attending a single lecture, Hunt was asked to leave the school. It must be noted that Hunt was accepted only to attend lectures, whereas the three blacks were admitted to the actual degree program. For Hunt's account, see her autobiography *Glances and Glimpses; or Fifty Years Social, Including Twenty Years Professional Life* (Boston: John P. Jewett, 1856; reprint ed., New York: Source Books, 1970), 214–218; for a modern perspective on the incident, see Mary Roth Walsh, *Doctor's Wanted: No Women Need Apply: Sexual Barriers in the Medical Profession, 1835–1975* (New Haven: Yale University Press, 1977), 25–33.

9. *Lily*, February 1851, 12.

10. *Una*, February 1854, 218.

11. *Una*, March 1854, 233–234.

12. *Una*, March 1854, 234.

13. For accounts of the numerous sects that evolved from differences of opinion over treatment and/or personality and that divided the medical profession into regular and eclectics, homeopaths, hydropaths, and others, see Martin Kaufman, *Homeopathy in America: The Rise and Fall of Medical Heresy* (Baltimore: Johns Hopkins University Press, 1971); and William Rothstein, *American Physicians in the Nineteenth Century: From Sects to Science* (Baltimore: Johns Hopkins University Press, 1972).

14. John Blake, "Women and Medicine in Ante-Bellum America," *Bulletin of the History of Medicine* 34 (March-April 1965): 117.

15. *Woman's Advocate*, April 19, 1856.

16. Walsh, *Doctors Wanted*, 186.

17. *Woman's Advocate*, November 29, 1856.

18. For accounts of women's work during the Civil War, see Mary Elizabeth Massey, *Bonnet Brigades* (New York: Knopf, 1966); and Ann Firor Scott, *The Southern Lady: From Pedestal to Politics 1830–1930* (Chicago: University of Chicago Press, 1970), 80–102.

19. *Revolution*, September 3, 1868, 133.

20. For background information on the history of women lawyers, see Karen Berger Morello, *The Invisible Bar: the Woman Lawyer in America: 1638 to the Present* (New York: Random House, 1986).

21. D. Kelly Weisberg, "Barred From the Bar: Women and Legal Education in the United States: 1870–1890," *Journal of Legal Education* 28 (1977):485–507.

22. In 1866 Lucy Hobbs Taylor became the first woman to receive the D.D.S. degree; see Ralph Edwards, "The First Woman Dentist: Lucy Hobbs Taylor, D.D.S.," *Bulletin of the History of Medicine* 25 (May–June 1951): 277–283.

23. *Revolution*, July 23, 1868, 37.

24. *Revolution*, December 31, 1868, 410.

25. *Agitator*, April 3, 1869, 5.

26. *Agitator*, July 3, 1869, 8.

27. *Agitator*, July 31, 1869, 8.

28. *Agitator*, September 11, 1869, 4.

29. *Agitator*, June 26, 1869, 5; October 23, 1869, 5.

30. *Agitator*, August 28, 1869, 1.

31. *Agitator*, September 25, 1869, 1.

32. *New Northwest*, July 7, 1871, 1.

33. *New Northwest*, December 26, 1878, 2.

34. *New Northwest*, January 2, 1879, 2.

35. *Queen Bee*, December 6, 1882, 1.

36. *Queen Bee*, September 26, 1883, 1.

37. *Queen Bee*, October 5, 1892, 1.

38. Walsh, *Doctors Wanted*, 180, 240.

39. *Woman's Journal*, February 5, 1870, 37.

40. *Woman's Journal*, March 13, 1880, 82.

41. *Woman's Journal*, May 7, 1881, 150–151.

42. Margaret Rossiter, *Women Scientists in America: Struggles and Stra**tegies to 1940* (Baltimore: Johns Hopkins University Press, 1982), 39.

43. *Woman's Journal*, July 19, 1879, 230.

44. *Woman's Journal*, June 25, 1870, 196.

45. *Woman's Journal*, July 16, 1875, 17; June 15, 1878, 188. For a

account of the reluctance of the Massachusetts Medical Society, the Pennsylvania State Medical Society, and the American Medical Association to admit women, see Martin Kaufman, "The Admission of Women to Nineteenth Century American Medical Societies," *Bulletin of the History of Medicine* 50 (Summer 1976): 251–260.

46. *Woman's Journal*, September 3, 1881, 281.

47. Walsh, *Doctors Wanted*, 108.

48. *Woman's Journal*, September 4, 1875, 281.

49. *Woman's Journal*, August 20, 1870, 264.

50. *Woman's Journal*, May 26, 1877, 167.

51. *Woman's Journal*, August 6, 1887, 250.

52. *Woman's Journal*, July 25, 1885, 234.

53. *Woman's Journal*, August 1, 1885, 248. For a brief account of American women students in Swiss medical schools, see Madelyn Holmes, "Go to Switzerland, Young Women, If You Want to Study Medicine," *Women's Studies International Forum* 7 (1984): 243–245.

54. Walsh, *Doctors Wanted*, 262.

55. Ruth Tryon, *Investment in Creative Scholarship: A History of the Fellowship Program of the American Association of University Women 1890–1956* (Washington, D.C.: American Association of University Women, 1957), 9.

56. *Woman's Journal*, June 30, 1888, 210. Benneson's letter also appeared in the *Woman's Tribune*, March 28, 1888.

57. *Woman's Journal*, January 19, 1889, 21. For details of the AAUW fellowship program between 1890 and 1956, see Tryon, *Investment in Creative Scholarship*.

58. Helen Ekin Starrett, *After College, What?* (New York: T.Y. Crowell, 1896), 5–19. For an account of the dilemmas experienced by women college graduates of the nineteenth century torn between the two spheres, see Joyce Antler, "After College, What?: New Graduates and the Family Claim," *American Quarterly* 32 (Fall 1980): 409–434. For biographical accounts of nine early professional women, see Penina Migdal Glazer and Miriam Slater, *Unequal Colleagues: the Entrance of Women into the Professions, 1890–1940* (New Brunswick, N.J.: Rutgers University Press, 1987).

59. For more detailed accounts of the triumph of "coercive philanthropy" at Johns Hopkins Medical School, see Rossiter, *Women Scientists*, 46–47; and Jacobi, "Woman in Medicine," in Meyer, *Woman's Work in America*, 204–205.

60. *Woman's Chronicle*, April 18, 1891, 1.

61. *Woman's Chronicle*, January 21, 1893, 2.

62. *Woman's Tribune*, August 1885, 4.

63. *Woman's Tribune*, May 14, 1892, 142.

64. Rosemary Stevens, *American Medicine and the Public Interest* (New Haven: Yale University Press, 1972), 116–118.

65. *Woman's Tribune*, January 19, 1889, 2.

66. *Woman's Tribune*, May 13, 1893, 86–87.

67. *Woman's Journal*, February 3, 1894, 37.

68. *Woman's Journal*, November 10, 1894, 358.

69. *Woman's Journal*, February 6, 1904, 46.

70. *Woman Citizen*, March 22, 1919, 904–905.

71. *Woman's Journal*, January 19, 1901, 17.

72. *Woman Citizen*, January 3, 1920, 666.

73. *Woman's Journal*, January 3, 1891, 5.

74. *Woman's Journal*, October 14, 1911, 326; *Woman Citizen*, August 31, 1918, 275.

75. *Woman's Journal*, July 14, 1891, 218.

76. *Woman's Journal*, May 12, 1900, 145.

77. *Woman's Journal*, June 17, 1916, 200; July 8, 1916, 219. For an account of women's lives in higher education see Geraldine Joncich Clifford, *Lone Voyagers: Academic Women in Coeducational Universities, 1869-1937* (New York: Feminist Press, 1989).

78. *Woman Citizen*, April 12, 1919, 976.

79. For accounts of her years at Harvard, see Hamilton's autobiography, *Exploring the Dangerous Trades* (Boston: Little, Brown, 1943), 252–267; and Barbara Sicherman, *Alice Hamilton: A Life in Letters* (Boston: Harvard University Press, 1984).

80. Janet Hooks, *Women's Occupations Through Seven Decades* (Washington, D.C.: U.S. Department of Labor, 1947; reprint ed., Washington, D.C.: Zenger Publishing Company, 1975), 158–159; 191–195.

81. Walsh, *Doctors Wanted*, 215. In support of the belief that the *Woman's Journal* abandoned women doctors is the fact that in 1903 a group of women doctors launched the *Woman's Medical Journal*, a monthly devoted to reporting issues of interest to women in medicine.

82. *Woman's Journal*, September 7, 1901, 284.

EPILOGUE

Utilizing a torrent of words, gallons of ink, and rolls of newsprint, women's rights activists witnessed, reported, and affected social change in papers of their own making. Appearing at a time when most women were isolated in their homes, with voices muted and minds restrained, the papers served as lively public arenas where women could interact, exchange vital information, discover role models, and recapture their self-esteem. In a world determined to restrict women's lives, to demean their mental and physical abilities, and to belittle their actions, the women's rights press publicly challenged society's deep-rooted beliefs about women's role and rights.

Popular newspapers and magazines of the period either ignored women or disparaged them and ladies' magazines supplied their readers with nothing more substantial than fashion advice, housekeeping hints, and entertaining fiction. Women's rights papers assumed the roles of women's spokespersons and supporters. They related women's concerns and accomplishments and articulated the goal of equality. The papers addressed the voluminous concerns of women, their legal, financial, social, and political rights, suffrage being the most well known of all of these. Within the early movement, women's right to higher education was a major goal and the papers orchestrated an intense campaign to achieve it. Contending that higher education was the foundation of women's equality, the papers vigorously promoted women's right to and role in higher education.

Each paper transmitted its views on women's higher education in a highly individualistic manner. Differences in presentation depended largely upon the editor's personal views about women's proper place in society. To the uninitiated the women's rights movement appeared as a cohesive body unified by the single-minded goal of achieving full equality for women. In reality, there existed within the movement a variety of philosophies and divergent opinions about women's proper role in society. The discord so common among women's rights activists about ends and methods found its way into their papers. Editors' sometimes confusing and quixotic views on women's higher education exemplified the lack of unity within the movement on a number of issues. Anne McDowell, editor of the antebellum *Woman's Advocate*, fought hard for women's right to be educated, but scorned her paper's designation as a women's rights title; Elizabeth Cady Stanton and the *Revolution* effusively urged women to learn a profession with frequent articles on the generous monetary rewards of such a career choice; Lucy Stone's *Woman's Journal* ardently championed coeducation and women's mental prowess but espoused many "true women" sentiments about the maternal duties of educated women and was often ambivalent about professional and public roles for women. The papers could not even resolve the question if it was better for women to be educated in a single-sex school or a coeducational institution.

The passage of time and rapidly changing social conditions also influenced how the papers reported on women's higher education. In the 1850s the *Lily* boldly mocked the female seminaries for their superficial curricula despite the fact they were the only institutions providing women with formal education. Sixty years later the *Woman's Journal* carried announcements of fellowships for women's graduate and professional education in universities here and abroad. Coverage of higher education issues disappeared altogether when the suffrage campaign intensified in the 1900s, showing the the women's movement had shifted its emphasis and focused on poltical rather than social issues.

Throughout the decades as each new hindrance to women's higher education arose, the papers deftly alerted readers to arguments used against their education and provided them with powerful counterarguments that could be used in their defense. Prior to the Civil War, women's rights papers had to contend with hazy generalization about women's lesser intellectual abilities. In the postwar years, arguments substantiated by ponderous scientific data detailed women's medical and biological incapacities for education; by the 1900s society was immersed in the emotional debate over "race suicide" and blamed the intellectual pursuits of educated women for deterring women from marital and maternal responsibilities. To thwart these ever-shifting obstacles, the women's rights press launched its own defense of women's right to and capacity for higher education. The papers marshaled their own legion of authoritative spokespersons and impressive arrays of scientific evidence to puncture the bombast of opponents and bolster women's claims to higher education.

Geography was another influence on how issues were or were not covered. The papers from the West, the *Pioneer* and the *Queen Bee*, were frustratingly mute on information on coeducation. The obvious explanation for this is that because so many western colleges were founded as coeducational institutions, the editors assumed that the problem was of no special interest to their readers. Based in Little Rock, Arkansas, the *Woman's Chronicle* was the most conservative of all the papers. It seldom engaged in reporting or commenting on anything inflammatory. Considering its location in the area of the nation most unsympathetic to women's rights issues, it is amazing that the paper even existed and spoke out as often as it did.

The papers had no single method for promoting women's higher education. They used every device possible—persuasion, coercion, humor, human interest stories, personal advice columns, even the words of well-known men when their message was supportive. They undertook a formidable task. Thomas Higginson, the stalwart champion of women's rights, likened women's higher education to "one of Spenser's palaces in the 'Faerie Queen,' that is guarded by a series of ghostly sentinels, all individually powerless as you approach, but collectively formidable to the imagination."[1] Women's rights papers were tireless forces in rendering the awesome sentinels powerless. They voiced the extraordinary concerns of middle-class women who in the process of creating a new version of womanhood deemed higher education to be an essential tool. Relaying the news of women's equality, the papers transmitted ideas, goals, and actions completely at odds with society's views about women.

To accurately measure the papers' influence is impossible. Although circulation figures were small—Bloomer boasted that the *Lily* had 6,000 subscribers in 1854, the *Revolution's* list never exceeded 3,000, and the *Woman's Journal* announced that it had 27,600 subscribers in 1916—there is no way to estimate how many individuals read each copy or even more significantly, how much a particular article or editorial influenced a reader to attend a college, apply for a fellowship, leave the teaching profession, or become a doctor or lawyer. Although the papers were aware that they would never have the polish or hefty subscription lists of the popular ladies' magazines, there is no denying that they considered themselves as change agents. In reflecting on her two-year association with the *Revolution*, Susan B. Anthony uncharacteristically stated:

No one but the good Father can ever begin to know the terrible struggle of those years. I am not complaining, for mine is but the fate of almost every originator or pioneer who has ever opened up a way. I have the joy of knowing that I showed it to be possible to publish an out-and-out woman's paper, and taught other women to enter in to reap where I have sown.[2]

Anthony and her sister editors knew that their papers played significant roles in transforming parlor-bound ladies into women with public voices and roles. The papers ended women's silence and submissiveness and helped women into directing and interpreting their lives, thoughts, and actions. For seven decades, women's rights papers relentlessly informed society that women should enjoy full participation in all aspects of American life, including higher education.

The papers left a sweeping saga of women's history told in women's words and from women's viewpoint. They provide fascinating insights into the myriad concerns and opinions of the early women's movement. Their emphasis on women's higher education illustrates that the movement considered a number of social goals and did not limit themselves solely to securing the vote for women. Evident from articles and editorials on higher education are the conflicting purposes, goals, and ambivalence on women's issues that characterized much of the early activists' words and actions. Also apparent are the middle-class origins and orientation of the movement. Nearly all of the editors and most of the readers were middle-class women and the issues the papers addressed were middle-class concerns.

This book focuses on a single issue among the multitude covered by the papers. This linkage of the history of women's higher education and women's rights papers, two overlooked facets of women's history, provides readers with new insights and fertile areas for additional research. By reading accounts of women's experiences in colleges and universities written by concerned women from all parts of the nation during a seventy-year period, one gains a rich and personal perspective of women's higher educational history and a deep appreciation for the tenacious fight waged by women to secure and maintain higher education for women.

A contemporary historian of the women's rights movement perceptively commented: "Not every educated woman was a rebel, but nearly every rebel had been educated."[3] Whereas women's rights activists never publicly advocated the concept of the educated rebel woman, it certainly was an implicit but unspoken part of all of their endeavors to secure higher education for women. Cognizant of the symbiotic relationship between higher education and women's equality, women's rights papers urged women to throw down their ladies' magazines and leave their parlors and boudoirs and seek higher education and the intellectual and personal benefits it engendered. By their melding of women's higher education to equality, women's rights papers made a significant impact on women's lives, the women's rights movement and on higher education. The compelling story of women's efforts to attain equality through higher education told in women's words and published in their own press is a legacy that should inspire women as they continue in their quest for equality in colleges and universities, the professions, and in their lives.

NOTES

1. Thomas Higginson, "Higher Education of Woman," in *The Liberal Education of Woman: the Demand and the Method*, ed. James Orton (New York: A.S. Barnes & Co., 1873), 309.

2. Elizabeth Cady Stanton and Harriot Stanton Blatch, *Elizabeth Cady Stanton*, 2 vols. (New York: Harper & Row, 1922), 2: 373.

3. Keith Melder, "The Beginnings of the Women's Rights Movement in the United States, 1800–1840," Ph.D. diss., Yale University, 1964, 123.

SELECTED BIBLIOGRAPHY

PRIMARY SOURCES

Agitator, 1869, Smith College Library, Northampton, Mass., on microfilm.

Lily, 1849–1856, Smith College Library, Northampton, Mass., on microfilm.

New Northwest, 1871-1887, Smith College Library, Northampton, Mass., on microfilm.

Pioneer, 1869–1873, Bancroft Library, University of California, Berkeley, on microfilm.

Queen Bee, 1882-1895, Colorado State Historical Society, Denver, on microfilm.

Revolution, 1868–1870, Smith College Library, Northampton, Mass., on microfilm.

Una, 1853–1855, Smith College Library, Northampton, Mass., on microfilm.

Woman's Advocate, 1855–1856?, Smith College Library, Northampton, Mass., on microfilm.

Woman's Chronicle, 1888–1893, Smith College Library, Northampton, Mass., on microfilm.

Woman's Journal/Woman Citizen, 1870–1932, Smith College Library, Northampton, Mass., on microfilm.

Woman's Tribune, 1883–1909, Smith College Library, Northampton, Mass., on microfilm.

SECONDARY SOURCES

Antler, Joyce. " 'After College, What?': New Graduates and the Family Claim." *American Quarterly* 32 (Fall 1980):409–434.

Barry, Kathleen. *Susan B. Anthony: a Biography of a Singular Feminist.* New York: New York University Press, 1989.

Bennion, Sherilyn Cox. "*The Pioneer*: the First Voice for Women's Suffrage in the West." *Pacific Historian* 25 (Winter 1981):15–21.

Bloomer, Dexter C. *Life and Writings of Amelia Bloomer.* Boston: Arena Press, 1895. Reprint. New York: Schocken, 1975.

Burstyn, Joan. *Victorian Education and the Ideal of Womanhood.* Totowa, N.J.: Barnes & Noble Books, 1980.

Churchill, Caroline Nichols. *Active Footsteps.* Colorado Springs: Mrs. C.N. Churchill Publisher, 1909.

Clifford, Geraldine Joncich. *Lone Voyagers: Academic Women in Coeducational Universities, 1869–1937.* New York: Feminist Press, 1989.

Conrad, Susan Phinney. *Perish the Thought: Intellectual Women in Romantic America, 1830–1860.* New York: Oxford University Press, 1976.

DuBois, Ellen. *Feminism and Suffrage: the Emergence of an Independent Women's Movement in America 1848–1869.* Ithaca: Cornell University Press, 1978.

Filene, Peter. *Him, Her, Self: Sex Roles in Modern America.* 2d ed. Baltimore: Johns Hopkins University Press, 1986.

Fox, Louis. "Pioneer Women's Rights Magazine." *New York Historical Society Quarterly* 42 (January 1958):71–74.

Frankfort, Roberta. *Collegiate Women: Domesticity and Career in Turn–of–the-Century America.* New York: New York University Press, 1977.

— Glazer, Penina Midgal and Miriam Slater. *Unequal Colleagues: the Entrance of Women into the Professions, 1890–1940.* New Brunswick, New Jersey: Rutgers University Press, 1987.

Griffith, Elisabeth. *In Her Own Right: the Life of Elizabeth Cady Stanton.* New York: Oxford University Press, 1984.

Hays, Elinor Rice. *Morning Star: a Biography of Lucy Stone 1818–1893.* New York: Harcourt, Brace, 1961.

— Hooks, Janet. *Women's Occupations Through Seven Decades.* Washington, D.C.: U.S. Department of Labor, 1947. Reprint. Washington, D.C.: Zenger Publishing Co., 1975.

— Horowitz, Helen. *Alma Mater: Design and Experience in the Women's Colleges from their Nineteenth–Century Beginnings to the 1930s.* New York: Knopf, 1984.

Livermore, Mary. *The Story of My Life in the Sunshine and Shadow of Seventy Years.* Hartford, Conn.: A.D. Worthington & Co., 1899.

Masel–Walter, Lynne. "A Burning Cloud by Day: the History and Content of the *Woman's Journal.*" *Journalism History* 3 (Winter 1976–1977):103–110.

———. "Their Rights and Nothing More: A History of the *Revolution,* 1868–1870." *Journalism Quarterly* 53 (Summer 1976):242–251.

———. "Their Rights and Nothing Less: the History and Thematic Content of the American Woman Suffrage Press, 1868–1920." Ph.D. diss., University of Wisconsin, 1977.

———. "To Hustle with the Rowdies: the Organization and Functions of the American Woman Suffrage Press." *Journal of American Culture* 3 (Spring 1980): 167–183.

Melder, Keith. *Beginnings of Sisterhood: the American Woman's Rights Movement, 1800–1850.* New York: Schocken Books, 1977.

———. "Woman's High Calling: the Teaching Profession in America, 1830–1860." *American Studies* 13 (Fall 1972):19–32.

Morello, Karen Berger. *The Invisible Bar: the Woman Lawyer in America: 1638 to the Present.* New York: Random House, 1986.

Mott, Frank Luther. *A History of American Magazines.* 5 vols. Cambridge: Harvard University Press, 1939–1968.

Moynihan, Ruth Barnes. *Rebel for Rights: Abigail Scott Duniway*. New Haven: Yale University Press, 1983.

Newcomer, Mabel. *A Century of Higher Education for American Women*. New York: Harper & Brothers, 1959.

Noun, Louise. "Amelia Bloomer: a Biography." Parts 1, 2. *Annals of Iowa* 47 (Winter, Spring 1985):575–617, 575–621.

Rosenberg, Rosalind. *Beyond Separate Spheres: Intellectual Roots of Modern Feminism*. New Haven: Yale University Press, 1982.

Rossiter, Margaret. *Women Scientists in America: Struggles and Strategies to 1940*. Baltimore: Johns Hopkins University Press, 1982.

Russett, Cynthia Eagle. *Sexual Science: the Victorian Construction of Womanhood*. Cambridge: Harvard University Press, 1989.

Ryan, Agnes. *The Torch Bearer, a Look Forward and Back at the Woman's Journal, the Organ of the Woman's Movement*. Boston: Woman's Journal and Suffrage News, 1916.

— Solomon, Barbara. *In the Company of Educated Women: a History of Women and Higher Education in America*. New Haven: Yale University Press, 1985.

Stanton, Elizabeth Cady, Susan B. Anthony, and Matilda Joslyn Gage, *History of Woman Suffrage*. 5 vols. New York: Fowler & Wells, 1881–1886.

Sterns, Bertha Monica. "Reform Periodicals and Female Reformers 1830–1860." *American Historical Review* 37 (July 1932):678–699.

— Taylor, James Monroe. *Before Vassar Opened: a Contribution to the History of the Higher Education of Women in America*. Boston: Houghton, Mifflin, 1914.

Thompson, Eleanor Wolf. *Education for Ladies 1830–1860: Ideas on Education in Magazines for Ladies*. New York: Kings Crown Press, 1947.

Walsh, Mary Roth. *Doctors Wanted: No Women Need Apply: Sexual Barriers in the Medical Profession, 1835–1975*. New Haven: Yale University Press, 1977.

Weisberg, D. Kelly. "Barred from the Bar: Women and Legal Education in the United States: 1870–1890." *Journal of Legal Education* 28 (1977):485–507.

Welter, Barbara. "Anti–Intellectualism and the American Woman: 1800–1860." *Mid–America* 48 (October 1966):258–270.

———. "The Cult of True Womanhood: 1820–1860." *American Quarterly* 18 (Summer 1966): 151–174.

———. *Dimity Convictions: the American Woman in the Nineteenth Century.* Athens, Ohio: Ohio University, 1976.

Woody, Thomas. *A History of Women's Education in the United States.* 2 vols. New York: Science Press, 1929. Reprint. New York: Octagon Press, 1966.

INDEX

About the Author

PATRICIA SMITH BUTCHER is Assistant Director of Readers Services at Trenton State College, New Jersey. She is the bibliographical editor of *Past and Promise, Lives of New Jersey Women* (Scarecrow, 1989). She has contributed articles and reviews to *History of Higher Education Annual, Library Journal,* and *RQ,* among others.